LOVE
AWAKENED
by LOVE

The Liberating Ascent of Saint John of the Cross

D1597003

LOVE AWAKENED by LOVE

The Liberating Ascent of Saint John of the Cross

MARK O'KEEFE, O.S.B.

ICS Publications
Institute of Carmelite Studies
Washington, D.C.

ICS Publications
2131 Lincoln Road NE
Washington, DC 20002-1199
800-832-8489
www.icspublications.org

Book and cover design and pagination by Rose Design

Produced and printed in the United States of America

Library of Congress Cataloging-in-Publication Data

O'Keefe, Mark, 1956–
  Love awakened by love : the liberating ascent of Saint John of the Cross / Mark O'Keefe, O.S.B.—1st [edition].
     pages cm
  Includes bibliographical references and index.
  ISBN 978-1-939272-15-7 (alk. paper)
  1. John of the Cross, Saint, 1542–1591. Subida del Monte Carmelo. 2. Mysticism—Catholic Church—Early works to 1800. 3. Spirituality—Catholic Church. 4. Spiritual life—Catholic Church. I. Title.
  BV5082.3.O37 2007
  248.2'2—dc23
                              2014003226

Other Books by Mark O'Keefe, O.S.B.

Deciding to Be Christian: A Daily Commitment
Liguori, 2012

Priestly Wisdom: Insights from St. Benedict
Abbey Press, 2004

Priestly Prayer: Reflections on Prayer in the Life of the Priest
Abbey Press, 2002

Priestly Virtues: Reflections on the Moral Virtues in the Life of the Priest
Abbey Press, 2000

*The Ordination of a Priest: Reflections on the Priesthood
in the Rite of Ordination*
Abbey Press, 1999

In Persona Christi: Reflections on Priestly Identity and Holiness
Abbey Press, 1998

*Becoming Good, Becoming Holy:
On the Relationship of Christian Ethics and Spirituality*
Paulist Press, 1995; St. Pauls/India, 1997; St. Pauls/Philippines, 1997

What Are They Saying About Social Sin?
Paulist Press, 1990

Translations and Abbreviations

Scripture quotations are from the *New Revised Standard Version Bible: Catholic Edition, Anglicized Text*, copyright © 1999, 1995, 1989, Division of Christian Education of the National Council of Churches of Christ of the United States of America. Used with permission. All rights reserved.

All quotations from the works of John of the Cross are taken from *The Collected Works of St. John of the Cross*, trans. Kieran Kavanaugh, O.C.D. and Otilio Rodriguez, O.C.D., rev. ed. (Washington, D.C.: ICS Publications, 1991).

Abbreviations for these works, as they appear in this book, are as follows:

A = *The Ascent of Mount Carmel*
C = *The Spiritual Canticle*
F = *The Living Flame of Love*
Lt = *Letters*
N = *The Dark Night*
Pre = *The Precautions*
SLL = *The Sayings of Light and Love*

References to particular texts within these works are indicated in the following way:

For *The Ascent of Mount Carmel* and *The Dark Night*, the first number indicates the book, the second number refers to the chapter, and the third number indicates the paragraph. For example, A.2.3.4 would refer to *The Ascent*, book 2, chapter 3, paragraph 4.

In a similar manner, for *The Spiritual Canticle* and *The Living Flame of Love*, the first number refers to the stanza and the second number to the paragraph. Thus, C.3.4 is a reference to the commentary on stanza 3, paragraph 4 of *The Spiritual Canticle*.

Contents

A Word of Thanks

I have been privileged to spend a month in each of the last three summers at the Centro Internacional Teresiano Sanjuanista (CITeS) in Avila, Spain. I am deeply grateful for the hospitality of the staff and the opportunity to draw on their superb resources. I was first introduced to CITeS through the fine summer Spanish-language program of the Institute of Spanish Language and Culture at the Catholic University of Avila.

My interest in and my understanding of John of the Cross have been enhanced by the opportunity to teach about his work and that of St. Teresa of Avila in Saint Meinrad Seminary and School of Theology. I am grateful for the interest, the questions, and the insights of my students.

I owe a debt of gratitude to those who have assisted me in the publication of the present work. In particular, I want to thank my confrere, Brother Francis Wagner, O.S.B., editor of the Path of Life Publications of my monastery's Abbey Press, who offered very helpful comments and recommendations about the text. I also wish to thank my editor at ICS Publications, Patricia Morrison, who was always speedy in her assistance, and for her contagious love for the great Carmelite mystics.

Preface

One of my university professors offered us students this advice: "Don't read good books!" He repeated it again: "Don't read good books!" and then added, "Read the best!" He went on to list the "best" books: Dante's *The Divine Comedy*, St. Augustine's *Confessions*, the tragedies and comedies of Shakespeare, the writings of St. John of the Cross, and many more. The professor added yet another imperative: "Find a good commentary on these works because the best books need dialogic partners."

We have in Father Mark O'Keefe's *Love Awakened by Love: The Liberating Ascent of Saint John of the Cross* a good dialogic partner. Father O'Keefe, as a moral theologian, presents a studied and prayerful commentary and analysis of one of the greatest spiritual Christian writers. John of the Cross is a spiritual mentor who continues to influence not only those within the Carmelite way of life but also countless individuals who are serious about their faith life. Because his writings are so deep and countercultural to our postmodern era, we benefit by a thoughtful and clear commentary.

What the reader will find in this volume are certain themes and convictions that Father O'Keefe unpacks for us. First and foremost is the focus on union with God. As creatures we have an infinite longing for intimacy, and St. John insists that nothing less than a share in God's very life will satisfy that hunger. We are made for oneness, and the God of love invites us into that intimacy.

A second major theme is liberation. In so many areas of our life we simply are not free. Enslavement to possessions or prestige, to power and pleasure, thwart our response to our deepest calling. St. John's writings help us to name those enslavements and to find our liberty in God's grace and a disciplined life of virtue. This theme of liberation presses upon us the seriousness of our Christian life. Only sacrifice and dedication will open our hearts to the workings of grace.

A third theme deals with an analysis of virtues and vices. Father O'Keefe's background in moral theology comes through as he speaks powerfully of St. John's insistence that only through a virtuous life can we ascend the mountain leading to God. This is true for both the moral virtues and the theological virtues of faith, hope, and charity. The strongest section of *Love Awakened by Love* comes in his commentary on the theological virtues.

My university professor insisted that we read primary sources. But he also had the wisdom to realize that students today often need guides who can interpret and provide a context for those primary sources. As anyone who reads the Bible knows, having a commentary at hand helps in both understanding and living out scriptural messages. Father O'Keefe helps us understand St. John's often dense and turgid works and motivates us to live out St. John's message of saying "yes" to God's invitation to love and to life, life to the full.

Most Reverend Robert Morneau
Auxiliary Bishop Emeritus of Green Bay
Green Bay, Wisconsin

Introduction

M any people have heard of St. John of the Cross, the great sixteenth-century Spanish Carmelite mystic and Doctor of the Church. Many of these same people have also probably begun to read one of his works in the hopes of gaining new spiritual insight. It is likely, however, that a good portion of those who have begun haven't finished the book they opened with such good intentions. Frankly, while the poetry of John of the Cross is sublime, his prose works are sometimes dense, and his spiritual teaching is demanding.

At the same time, others have probably picked up a work of John of the Cross because of their interest in contemplative prayer and Christian mysticism, and there is hardly a better spiritual master to consult. Yet, depending on the book with which they started, they found that he offered no techniques; and, in fact, John of the Cross devotes a great deal of attention to themes that seem to have very little to do with prayer, at least not directly—like the need to be purified, emptied, and dispossessed. Why, if you were looking for a resource to help you grow in the depth of your prayer, would you turn to a teaching that seems only tangentially related to it?

In this book it is my hope to introduce the thought of St. John of the Cross to those who have never heard of him or who know very little about him. I also want to offer a more welcoming introduction and broader orientation to those who might have tried to read him before but gave up. Finally, I hope to address those who are serious about growing into a deeper and more profound prayer life and relationship with God but do not yet fully understand the broader and more fundamental demands that this journey would require—requisites that have nothing directly to do with prayer. John of the Cross is a spiritual master who has a great deal to teach us—once we can place his thought in a context and understand some of his key concepts in more contemporary terms.[1]

Two Questions

But perhaps two questions might immediately occur to the reader of this book: why would a Benedictine like me have such an interest in the great Carmelite doctor? And what does a moral theologian, as I am, have to say about a master of the spiritual life?

What is a Benedictine doing writing about this Carmelite mystic? At one level, of course, that is a natural and even valid question, and some of my brother monks have asked me why I study and teach about the work of a Carmelite spiritual master when I come from a rich monastic spiritual heritage. In response to them, I recall one of our former abbots who had a great devotion to St. Joseph. When a monk challenged him, saying that he seemed to have a greater devotion to St. Joseph than to our Holy Father St. Benedict, our abbot replied, "There's no jealousy in heaven." True enough. More, of course, St. John of the Cross is a Doctor of the Church precisely because his teaching offers insight and truth to the entire church and to the spiritual tradition of every religious order—even one as venerable

---

1. There are a number of helpful general introductions to the thought of John of the Cross. See, especially, Kieran Kavanaugh, O.C.D., *John of the Cross: Doctor of Light and Love*, Spiritual Legacy Series (New York: Crossroad, 1999). Kavanaugh is one of the translators and editors of the collected works of John of the Cross, and his introduction in that text is brief but very helpful: *The Collected Works of St. John of the Cross*, trans. Kieran Kavanaugh, O.C.D., and Otilio Rodriguez, O.C.D., rev. ed. (Washington, D.C.: ICS Publications, 1999). A number of other useful introductions will be mentioned in the bibliography.

as the Benedictine tradition. There is no doubt that John was a fervent leader and son of the Carmelite reform in sixteenth-century Spain. He was profoundly formed by its rule and ideal, the lives of its saints, and its traditions. Yet what he has to teach every person who wants to draw closer to our God, even to the most intimate union with God in this life, transcends any particular school or family of Christian spirituality. Just as he insists that God ultimately transcends every concept or image that we might have, so too the path that John of the Cross shows can both embrace and ultimately transcend every particularity of distinct forms of Christian spirituality. I believe that I am living proof that one can be, for example, a proud and devoted son of St. Benedict (or the son or daughter of any other Christian spiritual tradition) and at the same time a disciple of this great Carmelite saint.

The second question: What does a moral theologian have to say about a master of spirituality? Well, of course, I write first as a Christian, interested in deepening my own life of prayer and discipleship and as a spiritual director who walks with others in their spiritual journey. In that sense, I am simply another reader who has benefited from John of the Cross, someone who is anxious to share the wonderful insights that I have found in his writings. Further, I am a moral theologian who is interested in the relationship of morality and spirituality—how the authentic Christian moral life must be nourished by our spiritual lives and how, as the Christian tradition has always held, an authentic spiritual life is built on a good Christian moral life. Really, the two are inseparable; morality and spirituality are two distinct but inseparable elements of the one Christian life. John of the Cross was profoundly aware of this truth, though it was not his concern to frame the issue in that way. In fact, as the reader will see, my specific perspective and framework for understanding the teachings of John of the Cross will often be those of the traditional Catholic moral theologian that I am.

The particular focus of this general introduction is on what John has to say about what he calls purgation or what he refers to as purifying, darkening, emptying—that is, I intend to reflect on the process of freeing ourselves, with God's help, from the sin, the blindness, and the various other forms of personal enslavement that prevent us from responding fully and generously to God's amazing self-offer to us in Christ. John's insights in this area are demanding and rich. As a moral theologian, I would call this same process "liberation"—the inner liberation that is utterly essential so that we can be truly free to love God (and neighbor) as we ought and as we truly desire, and so that we can be open to the love and the communion that the God of Jesus wants to give us. John of the Cross lays out before us a path of conversion and freedom to accept and respond to God's self-offer. One well-known Spanish commentator on the works of the Carmelite saint concludes that his *The Ascent of Mount Carmel* in particular could aptly be called a "great hymn to liberty of spirit." In fact, it could just as well be titled "From Slavery to the Liberty of the Children of God."[2]

Although the present study looks broadly at the Christian journey as described by John of the Cross, at its heart are the three chapters devoted to his discussion of the three theological virtues of faith, hope, and love. The Catholic tradition has provided a rich teaching about the important role of these three fundamental virtues in the Christian life (though perhaps these virtues have not always been consistently and effectively exemplified by Christian men and women). One of the chapters that

2. José Damián Gaitán, "Subida del Monte Carmelo," in *Introducción a la lectura de San Juan de la Cruz*, ed. Salvador Ros García (Salamanca, Spain: Junta de Castilla y León, 1993), 394–95.

follows will summarize some of these traditional insights, but at the same time, while drawing on the tradition, John of the Cross offers a distinctive and valuable perspective. For him, faith, hope, and love are gifts of God as well as instruments of what I am calling an inner liberation, given to us precisely so that we can be ready to receive the gift of contemplative prayer that God wants to give. In this way, John of the Cross offers us a critical tool for the deepening of the Christian life, yet his teaching in this area is little discussed in commentaries on his thought, at least not in English. To understand his thinking on these virtues, it is necessary to see how these three virtues function within the context of the broader work of liberation that must first occur within the Christian and that must continue into a still deeper purification. So the chapters that precede the discussions of faith, hope, and love as well as the chapters that follow them provide both an essential context and a broad overview of the entire spiritual itinerary as John of the Cross understands it. In the terms of John of the Cross, my focus is on what he would called the "active nights of sense and spirit," the specific emphasis of his *The Ascent of Mount Carmel*—but precisely in the context of the whole of his thought.

Why Read John of the Cross Today?

The Christian tradition has been blessed with many superb teachers and examples of deep prayer, sanctity, and faithful discipleship. In that sense, St. John of the Cross is one among many of our ancestors in the faith who illuminate the Christian path for us. At the same time, because we live in a different time and culture, their writings can contain expressions and even whole frameworks of understanding that are different from our own. Even while we acknowledge that these classics surely contain great treasures for our journey even today, those spiritual riches might seem relatively inaccessible to us because of the need to translate, not only in the sense of language to language, but also from one way of framing and expressing ideas to another. Such is certainly the case with at least many parts of the prose works of John of the Cross. He was a man well versed in the Scholastic philosophy and theology of his time, its philosophical underpinnings, conceptual framework, terms, and ways of expression. In short, as many have found, it is difficult at times for contemporary readers to fully grasp his analysis without some further explanation or context.

It is a fundamental presupposition of the present work that the writings of John of the Cross are well worth the effort that it might require to unlock their treasures—not to mention the fact that there is so much "low-hanging fruit" to be savored even if the reader were never to grasp all of the spiritual wisdom that he has to offer. John of the Cross is a universal Doctor of the Church for good reason. He offers one of the first true systematic presentations of Christian mystical theology, drawing on multiple resources to describe, explain, and analyze the experience and path of deepening prayer. In the last five hundred years, countless women and men who were already advanced in the ways of prayer have found in his teaching a way of understanding their experience. Certainly, even more individuals, beginners in prayer, have benefitted from his presentation of the path that lies ahead—its pitfalls, obstacles, and demands—so that they can set out in earnest. His poetry especially serves for God-seekers (at whatever point they are on the journey) as a constant reminder of the sublime invitation that God holds out for us all.

In our society today, perhaps more than ever, we want what we want, and we want it now. We might not be wealthy, but we often have fairly easy access to much of what we desire. With ever better technologies to make everything easier for us, we are accustomed not to have to struggle to enjoy what we want. We even want prayer without effort and without discipline. Well, to desire easy prayer is natural enough; to expect it is quite another matter. We want good "prayer experiences," good feelings in prayer. But, as we have all learned, if one's prayer depends on how it feels, we probably won't stick with it for very long because feelings in prayer come and go.

In fact, John of the Cross is simply a particularly focused and unflinching spokesperson for the long Christian spiritual tradition that teaches us at least two important things: first, that true, deep prayer and union with God normally come only to those whose lives have become fertile ground for the gift of true contemplation; and second, that feelings and "experience" in prayer are virtually no authentic measure whatsoever of the quality or depth of real prayer. In offering spiritual counsel to a group of nuns, for example, John cautions them: "Never set eyes on the pleasant feelings found in spiritual exercises, becoming attached to them and carrying on these practices only for the sake of this satisfaction. Nor should such a person run from the bitterness that may be found in them" (Pre 17).

In prayer, we are seeking a deeper communion with God. We want union with God—the uniting of our hearts, minds, and wills with God. But how can we hope to attain such union when our daily lives are, in fact, inconsistent with God's will and God's ways? How could we be fertile ground for the contemplation that is ultimately a gift from God if we have not prepared the ground, emptied the vessel, or cleaned the house? How can we be conformed to God in prayer if our minds in conscious thoughts, our wills in the choices we make, and the desiring that moves us are not, at the same time, being conformed to God? This is just another way of expressing what John of the Cross has to say about purgation—exterior and interior—in the senses and in the spirit.

With keen insight into our humanity, sinful and graced, John lays out the tasks that lie ahead for someone who really wants to be disposed for deep union with God—rather than one who is just seeking good experiences in prayer from time to time.

We don't think much about asceticism these days—not so much in the sense of doing penance for our sins but in the much richer and positive sense of engaging in the struggle to be conformed to God, the effort to free ourselves of everything or anything that keeps us from attaining deep union with God. John of the Cross is no masochistic dualist, a vestige of some bygone spiritual tradition now transcended. No, he is a particularly focused and clear spokesperson for a deep truth that has been experienced by centuries of saints, officially canonized or not. The truth is that we are sinners who must engage actively, with God's help, in a daily work of conversion. True contemplation and union with God are normally gifts that rain upon and bear fruit in ground that has been made ready by the hard work of the one who diligently and faithfully cultivates one's mind and heart.

John of the Cross also addresses our natural desire for good experiences and good feelings in prayer. For beginners in prayer (which is most of us, at some level), feelings of devotion and an active sense of God's presence are important to keep us faithful to prayer. But spiritual feelings come and go. We will not be faithful to prayer in any regular way if our fidelity is based on something as transitory as feelings. In fact, as our tradition tells us, sometimes the best prayer is dry prayer—prayer that is offered to God without the reward of superficial feeling, prayer that is built on faith that God's truest work occurs at a level deeper than anything that we could experience in an ordinary sense of that word. Here John of the Cross stands in a long tradition—though perhaps he is bolder and more firm than others—in teaching that the true and living God transcends not only our feelings but also our images, our concepts, our ideas, or even the narrow constraints of what can be contained in the truest of doctrines. Authentic, deep encounter with this living and transcendent God is always beyond what our senses can grasp, though God is always seeking to draw us nearer in prayer and in daily life. In the end, the sign of good prayer is not warm feelings in prayer but the fruit that our prayer bears in our daily living: Are we more generous, forgiving, humble, selfless, and loving? If the answer to this question is yes, then we have good reason to believe that our prayer is deepening even if it is as dry as a bone.

In the end, we should read John of the Cross today because he sings of the unfathomable depth and breadth of God's love for us. He shows us the way to allow ourselves to become truly open, profoundly empty, and finally free to receive and respond to the divine self-giving. We should read this great mystic today because he speaks a profound truth that perhaps we sometimes wish were not so: responding to the self-offering of a transcendent God and an invitation into the divine life demands a total commitment on our part. This is nothing more than what Jesus says when he challenges us to love God with our entire being. As soon as we try to live up to that challenge, we discover immediately how right John of the Cross is. For sinful human beings, engaging in that kind of love for God is mighty hard work—in fact, it is a long process that requires God's superabundant help—not unlike a steep climb up a mountain.

A Companion

I hope that the present work will serve as an introduction and invitation to enter into the amazing spiritual richness and depth that St. John of the Cross has to offer. I hope that the reflections that follow will encourage readers to delve into his works or return to them again if this is not their first encounter with him. Perhaps precisely because I am not an academic specialist in spirituality or a Carmelite, who might have long, personal experience of the topic and the tradition, my reflections will speak in a profitable way to other readers like myself. I came to John of the Cross with the same less specialized tools and presuppositions that characterize a majority of those who try to draw out the genuine treasure that is the spiritual theology of this great Doctor of the Church. At the same time, I do come with the eyes of a moral theologian whose discipline is the necessary companion to the study of spirituality—at least as the Christian way has been understood by the long tradition of which John of the Cross is a particularly insightful and valuable mentor and witness.

At one level, as a general introduction to the thought of St. John of the Cross, this book does have a particular focus. As I have said, the heart of this work is John's thought about the work of purgation—interior and exterior—carried on with God's help. The focus, then, is on what John calls the *active nights* of sense and of spirit, which he discusses in *The Ascent of Mount Carmel*. To understand this phase of the Christian journey requires an understanding of the broader path and the goal to which it leads, so we cannot neglect to speak of that further work of liberation that is more properly God's work, the so-called *passive* nights of sense and of spirit that lead into the deepest union with the triune God. At the same time, because of my particular focus I will not address topics that are more proper to a mystical theology such as, for example, the various stages or types of union, the experience of extraordinary phenomena, or the nature of mystical knowing.[3]

---

3. On mystical knowing, see Edward Howells, *John of the Cross and Teresa of Avila: Mystical Knowing and Selfhood* (New York: Crossroad, 2002).

Perhaps the present work is best understood as a general invitation to explore John of the Cross and his works as well as, more particularly, a companion to—rather than a commentary on—*The Ascent of Mount Carmel*. In what follows I intend to offer notes somewhat sparingly, simply to point to possibilities for further reading and to indicate the source of some distinctive perspective. A select bibliography offers some broader recommendations for further study. It is my hope that the present book will introduce John's insights into the graced work of liberation that can allow us to enter into that depth of mutuality with God that, for John of the Cross, is the only goal worthy of the Christian life.

For Questions for Reflection / Discussion see page 151

1 The Life and Spiritual Itinerary of St. John of the Cross

The parents of the future St. John of the Cross, Gonzalo de Yepes and Catalina Alvarez, married for love—Gonzalo was from a wealthy family of cloth merchants; Catalina was a weaver from a poor family.[1] Against the conventions of the time and with the threat that Gonzalo would be disinherited by his wealthy family, they married in 1529. In so doing, Gonzalo left behind the relatively comfortable life that he had most probably known as well as the successful future that he could legitimately have expected. Instead poverty and hardship followed; and sixteen years later, Gonzalo died, leaving Catalina with three young sons, Francisco, Luis, and Juan (John). Luis died two years later, probably of illness related to malnutrition. Still, despite hardships, Catalina maintained her deep faith, reaching out to people around her who were even more unfortunate than her little family was.

---

1. A brief but helpful biography and a chronology of major dates in the life of John of the Cross is provided by Kieran Kavanaugh, O.C.D., in his general introduction to *The Collected Works of St. John of the Cross*, trans. Kieran Kavanaugh, O.C.D., and Otilio Rodriguez, O.C.D., rev. ed. (Washington, D.C.: ICS Publications, 1999), 9–33; hereafter cited as *The Collected Works*. The classic modern biography is Crisógono de Jesús Sacramentado, *Vida y obras completas de San Juan de la Cruz*, 7th ed. (Madrid: Biblioteca de Autores Cristianos, 1973). In English translation it is *The Life of St. John of the Cross*, trans. Kathleen Pond (London: Longmans, Green, 1958). For a more contemporary biography, see Richard Hardy, *John of the Cross: Man and Mystic* (Boston: Pauline, 2004). A massive (900-plus pages) new biography in Spanish was recently published by noted sanjuanist scholar José Vicente Rodríguez: *San Juan de la Cruz: La biografía* (Madrid: San Pablo, 2012).

These simple facts show us the context in which the future St. John of the Cross was formed as a child. To surrender all for love and to show love for one's brothers and sisters became essential elements of the life and spiritual vision of the saint and Doctor of the Church who has rightly been called the "Doctor of Mystical Love."[2]

A brief review of some major biographical and historical details will help us to know John of the Cross as a person and to understand better the richness of his thought. After a few words about his published works, we will offer a broad overview of the spiritual path as John presented it, in order to place in proper context what follows in the chapters to come. We will then conclude the present chapter with some things to keep in mind as one reads St. John of the Cross, especially for the first time.

A Life in Context, and a Context to Understand a Vision

Unlike St. Teresa of Avila, his co-worker in the Carmelite reform and fellow Doctor of the Church, John of the Cross left no autobiographical works, only a handful of extant letters, and virtually no explicit autobiographical references in his published works. Much of what we know about his life comes from those who knew him, and many of the details have undoubtedly been embellished to meet the hagiographical style of the time with its emphasis on miracles and extraordinary mystical experiences. Still, we know a good deal about his life, and his character and religious vision shine out in those of his writings that are available to us.

2. This connection is made by Daniel Chowning, O.C.D., "Free to Love: Negation in the Doctrine of John of the Cross," in *John of the Cross*, ed. Steven Payne, O.C.D., Carmelite Studies 6 (Washington, D.C: ICS Publications, 1992), 29–47.

John was born in 1542 in the province of Avila.[3] It was the Golden Age of Spain, the *Siglo de Oro*, the "Golden Century," a period of great dynamism and change as the Spanish empire expanded across the globe.[4] Only fifty years earlier, in 1492, Columbus had discovered the Americas and opened the period of Spanish expansion and colonization. In that same year, King Ferdinand of Aragon and Queen Isabella of Castile, who through their marriage had united the two major kingdoms of what makes up modern-day Spain, defeated the last Moorish kingdom in Spain, centered in Granada, ending seven hundred years of Moorish presence and domination on the Iberian Peninsula. Also in 1492, in a decision that we see quite differently from a contemporary perspective, Spanish Jews were expelled or forced to convert to Christianity in an effort to bring religious unity to a newly geographically unified Christian kingdom. For Spain, it was a time of great dynamism and expectation.

No less was it a time of religious renewal and spiritual fervor. The winds of reform were blowing throughout Europe, and the Council of Trent and the beginning of the Catholic Counter-Reformation were only a few years away. Ferdinand and Isabella and their immediate successors were advocates of this reforming spirit, and they set out to promote renewal of the clergy, men and women religious, and church institutions in Spain. At the same time, this spirit of renewal had already taken hold in many religious orders, with an emphasis on returning to the spirit of their founders, to contemplation, and to poverty. With Spanish

---

3. Despite the location of his birth, John of the Cross is not to be confused with another recently proclaimed Spanish Doctor of the Church, St. John of Avila. Though roughly a contemporary and also a notable spiritual writer, the latter was a diocesan priest whose principal pastoral work was carried out in southern Spain.

4. For a superb introduction to St. John of the Cross in his historical context, see Federico Ruiz, O.C.D., ed., et al., *God Speaks in the Night: The Life, Times, and Teaching of St. John of the Cross*, trans. Kieran Kavanaugh, O.C.D. (Washington, D.C.: ICS Publications, 1991).

colonial expansion, together with its more sinister realities, there was a zeal for evangelization that mingled with the reforming spirit. Although the printing press was barely a hundred years old, theological and spiritual writings from Europe were flooding into Spain and being translated into Spanish, and spiritual writers and publications written in the vernacular abounded in Spain.

With this spirit of general religious fervor, there was a growing interest in prayer. Religious from reformed orders, especially Franciscans, were encouraging and teaching the prayer of quiet recollection even to lay people. Beyond mere formalism and printed prayers, there was interest in a more affective prayer and ultimately in contemplative prayer. Perhaps it was inevitable in a period before the Council of Trent established the seminary system, when clergy were poorly trained and the laity often barely catechized, that excesses and problems would arise. Misguided efforts and excessive focus on extraordinary mystical experiences led some groups into types of belief that were incompatible with sound Christian doctrine (such as the *Alumbrados*, "illuminated ones"). The Inquisition, originally established in Spain to root out suspected Jewish practices among recent converts from Judaism (*conversos*), came to focus on these various forms of false mysticism.[5] Thus, even while interest in the prayer of recollection grew, there was, at the same time, suspicion of all such interest and a call to return exclusively to pious external religious practices and vocal prayer.

This is the world into which Juan de Yepes was born. Although tremendous wealth had already begun to flow into Spain, much of

---

5. The probable Judeo-Christian (*converso*) heritage of John's paternal family has been a topic of much research and discussion. Rodríguez, referring to the most recent research in his new biography, affirms this probability (*San Juan de la Cruz*, 72–74). In sixteenth-century Spain, with its heightened concern for purity of family lineage and "honor," a Jewish family background could have serious social and even ecclesiastical consequences.

it went to fight foreign wars, and the general economic situation of simple folk within Spain actually grew more precarious. John's little family lived in poverty, ultimately in an important center of trade at the time, Medina del Campo. His mother continued her work as a weaver. Still, John was fortunate. He grew up in a loving and faith-filled home, and he was able to begin his education in a local school for the poor and orphans. It was there that he tried his hand at various trades, with the thought of becoming an apprentice for future work, but he did not prove adept at any of them (though many of these skills probably proved useful when, as a Carmelite superior, he personally helped with the order's building projects and maintenance). Noticing the young boy's gentleness and piety, the administrator of a hospital for the poor chose John to act as a kind of orderly and to go out to petition alms to support the hospital. The young boy proved to be a compassionate and attentive caregiver, and later in life he showed particular solicitude for the sick and the poor.

Hoping that John might one day become the chaplain of the hospital, the administrator arranged for the gifted young man to enter a new Jesuit school where he was fortunate to receive a classical education. This formation provided a solid base for the work of the future poet, writer, and preacher. But John's future was not as a hospital chaplain. In 1563 he entered the Carmelites, taking the name John of St. Matthias. He does not record why he chose this order over the many others in Medina del Campo, but it might well have been because of the order's contemplative roots and its devotion to the Virgin Mary.

John was sent to the University of Salamanca to study philosophy and theology. It was one of the oldest and most prestigious universities in Europe; and, at the time of John's studies, it was flourishing, gifted with renowned scholars from the many religious orders who provided the faculty of the great university. It was a time of rich intellectual ferment, and John was introduced to a number of diverse contemporary theological trends, including the thought of both St. Thomas Aquinas and St. Bonaventure, among others. John proved to be a gifted student, but he was experiencing a deeper discontent, longing for a life that was more contemplative than seemed possible in the academic life of a university or even in the Carmelite order of the time. He seriously pondered entering the far more austere and contemplative order, the Carthusians. Then he met St. Teresa of Avila.

Teresa of Jesus, as she was more properly known, had only recently established her first reformed Carmelite community of nuns in nearby Avila. And in 1567, at the time that the newly ordained John had come to Medina del Campo for his first Mass, she arrived to set up a second community of her reform. At the same time, she was also on the lookout for Carmelite friars to begin a reformed men's community, a project for which she had just received permission. The serious and gifted young Friar John was recommended to her, and on meeting Teresa, he told her about his idea of entering the Carthusians. She, for her part, shared her vision for a return to the primitive Carmelite rule with its emphasis on contemplation, silence, and poverty; and she convinced the young priest that he should seek the more contemplative life that he desired within the newly reformed Order of Mount Carmel rather than look elsewhere. His "novitiate" took place in the following year when he accompanied Teresa and a group of her nuns to make another foundation of nuns of the reform. In that year, 1568, he took the much simpler habit of the reform and changed his name to John of the Cross.

In 1567, at the time of their first meeting, Teresa of Jesus was fifty-two years old. John was twenty-five. She was, by then, advanced in the spiritual life, having already received mystical graces, and she had written two of her major works, *The Life* and *The Way of Perfection*. She had read a great deal about the life of prayer and consulted with many learned and spiritual people. St. Teresa was a woman with a vision of reform, zeal for her calling, and the drive and charisma to attain what she believed God wanted of her. John too was already advanced in prayer, though he left no record of the progress of his spiritual life, as did Teresa. Small in stature, he was bright, talented, and zealous for the life of prayer. He would learn from her the spirit of the Carmelite reform, probably tempering too his youthful fervor so that he could become the demanding but compassionate superior that he was later known to be. The Teresian reform would be unbending in its commitment to the Carmelite ideal but, at the same time, moderate (by the standards of the time) and humane. Eventually, for a time, John became Teresa's confessor and spiritual guide, but it is impossible to say how they mutually influenced and taught one another. Teresa brought a great of deal of experience and self-reflection; John certainly brought the theological and analytical gifts to provide a more systematic presentation of the spiritual vision that they largely shared.

In 1572, after working with other friars to begin the reform among the male branch of the order in several locations, John arrived to serve as confessor at the Monastery of the Incarnation in Avila, where Teresa had spent much of her religious life and where she had now been named prioress. There he began in earnest the work of spiritual guidance, particularly of women, that would mark his ministry for the rest of his life, as his extant letters and the testimony of his contemporaries attest. It was during this time that St. Teresa received the mystical gift of spiritual marriage, the highest level of union with God.

Unfortunately, tension had arisen between the members of the Carmelite reform (called "discalced," meaning "without shoes," though in fact they wore sandals) and those of the traditional observance (the "calced"). The speed with which the reform was spreading was a concern to the other Carmelites. Questions of ecclesiastical jurisdictions and a changing flow of principal players led to a situation of charged controversy. In December of 1577, John was abducted from the chaplain's lodgings at the Monastery of the Incarnation and was carried away to a secret imprisonment at the monastery of the Carmelite friars of the ancient observance in Toledo. There he was urged to recant his commitment to the reform and to accept the jurisdiction of these Carmelite superiors. During his imprisonment, John was subjected to great cruelty: regular beatings, rations consisting only of bread and water, and solitary confinement in a narrow, squalid room with only a tiny slit high up on the wall to allow the entrance of fresh air. In the winter his cell was freezing cold; in the summer the heat was suffocating. The temptation to feel completely alone and abandoned must have been great.

Amazingly, in the midst of these hardships, given a pen, ink, and some paper by one of his kinder jailers, John of the Cross began to write some of the world's most beautiful mystical poetry, including a major portion of *The Spiritual Canticle*. Here we find a parallel between his external experience and a cornerstone of his spiritual doctrine: that we find God most profoundly in darkness and obscurity, a God who is intimately present to us although we cannot discern this divine presence with our ordinary senses. One dark night, in August 1578, John managed to escape from his imprisonment and return to the safety of the discalced Carmelites. The details of his escape—secretly loosening the bolts of his cell door, tying together pieces of cloth to serve as rope, lowering himself out a window onto a wall below, and more—are worthy of a great adventure novel. How much of this experience of darkness and escape, physical and spiritual, is contained in the openings stanza of his exquisite poem *The Dark Night*?

> One dark night,
> fired with love's urgent longings
> —ah, the sheer grace!—
> I went out unseen,
> my house being now all stilled.

The tension between the branches of the Carmelite order was resolved in 1580 with their separation into different jurisdictions (and more definitively in 1593, after John's death, when the Discalced Carmelites became a separate order). John went on to a variety of assignments on behalf of the reform. In fact, the next thirteen years, from the time of his escape until his death, were very active ones: founding new monasteries, serving in both local and provincial leadership and administration, making visitations at discalced houses, and participating in the other business of the order. A good deal of this activity required regular travel between the monasteries, long and arduous journeys, given the travel conditions of the time and extremes of weather. As superior, John proved to be strict but at the same time prudent and even kindhearted. He showed particular personal attention to sick confreres and to those in need. He assisted humbly with practical labors such as constructing monasteries, cloisters, and aqueducts—with skills, no doubt, that he had learned decades earlier in that school for the poor and orphans.

From the beginning, the discalced friars, unlike their female counterparts, left their monasteries to preach, and John had an active preaching ministry. Wherever he was assigned, he spent many hours offering spiritual guidance, both in person and by letter. He offered his developing spiritual doctrine to his friars, the nuns, as well as to devoted laity. It is precisely this ministry that became the source of the writings we have today. John's major prose writings are commentaries on his poetry—part commentary, part spiritual treatise—to explain to those under his spiritual direction the mystical path contained in his verse. In that sense, his writings are themselves a form of spiritual guidance for those who hungered for more but had no guides to help them walk this often dark and obscure path.

Through all of these many and diverse activities, John dedicated hours to prayer. He often took the friars out for long walks in nature, and he would go off alone, to be found hours later in deep prayer. His friars reported finding him, many times, rapt in prayer and staring out a window, facing a starry sky. His poetry is surely a window into this experience—and sometimes even an account of it, in rich poetic form—even if he left no personal narrative record of his experiences of prayer and mystical gifts as did St. Teresa of Avila.

Sadly, in his final years, as much as he tried to avoid it, John found himself caught up in disputes within the still-young Carmelite reform. In 1590 he fell into disfavor with the discalced provincial and was on the verge of being sent off to a Carmelite mission planned for Mexico or even expelled from the order. He became seriously ill, suffering from infections related to sores in his foot. On December 14, 1591, at age forty-nine, John of the Cross died in Ubeda in southern Spain. His remains were ultimately transferred to Segovia, north of Madrid, where he had served as prior. They remain there today. His books began to appear in print only in 1618. He was canonized in 1726 and named a Doctor of the Church in 1926.

The Writings

St. John of the Cross is recognized as one of the great poets of the Spanish language, although only a few of his poetic works remain. Undoubtedly, the Jesuits in their school in the childhood home of the saint, Medina del Campo, provided much of the classical and literary foundation for his skill. In addition, John has left four major prose works: *The Ascent of Mount Carmel, The Dark Night, The Spiritual Canticle,* and *The Living Flame of Love.*[6]

The Ascent of Mount Carmel and *The Dark Night* are basically a two-volume work that describes the spiritual journey as a series of purgations—a purifying or progressive liberation—that culminates, by God's gift, in the transformation of the human person through union with God. Both texts are focused on the same poem, *The Dark Night. The Ascent* begins as a commentary on the poem but quickly becomes a treatise related to the content of the poem. For reasons not entirely known to us, the work ends rather abruptly, apparently unfinished. *The Dark Night* retains a bit more of the structure of a commentary, but it ultimately discusses only two of the poem's eight stanzas. In the chapters that follow, we will focus a good deal of our attention on the content of *The Ascent.*

The Spiritual Canticle and *The Living Flame of Love* are commentaries on the poems of the same names. Both are focused on the experience of union itself. In their more uplifting and even soaring spirit, we can place the sometimes arduous feel of the two previous works into their fuller context. It must be remembered that John of the Cross wrote all of these works within a relatively short span of years. He didn't take up his writing

---

6. The basic chronology of John's writings is summarized by Kavanaugh in his introduction to *The Collected Works*, 34–35. A biographical chronology is provided on pages 28–33 of the same work.

ministry until he had long completed his theological studies, was himself already well advanced in the spiritual life, and had gained a rich experience through directing others. Thus, even his reflections on and analysis of the arduous path through the purifications were written from the vantage point of someone who had actually passed through them. In this sense, one does not find in these works the significant development of thought that one often finds in the works of those who write over more years, whose experience is still unfolding, or whose thought is still developing. There is, for example, a notable development from St. Teresa's *Life*, begun in 1562, to her crowning masterpiece, *The Interior Castle*, completed in 1577.

In addition to these major works of John, a few letters have been preserved. There is an interesting and rich collection of very brief spiritual counsels that have been compiled with the title *The Sayings of Light and Love*. These were little sayings that John would write on a piece of paper to give to individual friars and nuns to remind them of his spiritual counsel, something akin to the pithy sayings of the desert fathers and mothers. Some of these sayings have come down to us in autograph form. Finally, there are three brief documents that John wrote regarding very specific situations. All of these briefer works contain valuable insights and sometimes profound counsels.

In his prose works, John of the Cross provides one of the first examples of a truly systematic spiritual or mystical theology. He drew on many sources to provide a theological understanding of deep spiritual experience and of the Christian journey more broadly. His debt to the Scholastic tradition that he had studied at Salamanca is clear, as will be attested in the chapters that follow. However, he was not afraid to draw on other theological sources, sometimes in an eclectic manner, in order to explain an obscure point. His devotion to Scripture is clear and consistent, and he intends to base his reflections on its wisdom (A.Prol.2). His biblical quotations are abundant. His method of scriptural interpretation is not the same as ours, but it is rich and seeks the deeper, "hidden" meaning of the texts beneath the literal. He placed his interpretations under the teaching of the church. John's dependence on other authors, particularly other mystical authors, is not clear. He quotes others infrequently, but, as we have seen, foreign theological and mystical works, in translation, had been virtually flooding into Spain (though slowed by the suspicions of the Inquisition). Thus, it is likely that he had read many of the writings of Spanish and foreign mystical writers in circulation in his day. Certainly, one of the greatest sources for his theology was experience—his own, certainly, but also that of the many people whom he had guided, especially Teresa of Avila. In the end, it is no exaggeration to say that the written works of John of the Cross are truly classics, masterpieces of spiritual theology.

The Spiritual Itinerary

To speak of the Christian life using the analogy of travel or dynamic movement is commonplace throughout our tradition. Growth in prayer and living discipleship more faithfully is like a journey, a path, a pilgrimage. One classic framework with which to speak of this dynamism in the Christian life is called the "Three Ways," which describes development from beginner through proficient to perfect (or, in other terms, as the purgative, illuminative, and unitive ways). John of the Cross was certainly familiar with this concept and refers to it in his works, but it is not really an organizing principle of his thought as it would be in spiritual works of later centuries.

The image of a journey or path is perhaps clearest in the title of one of his major works, *The Ascent of Mount Carmel*. Of

course, the choice of this particular term suggests that this journey is an uphill climb. His explanation of his famous diagram of
Mount Carmel by which he encapsulates his spiritual doctrine—
and which he has placed at the beginning of *The Ascent*—has at
its center the sure and speedy path that leads to the summit.[7] As
direct as this path might be, it is nonetheless an often arduous
journey that takes the person from sin to divine union.

At the same time, in addition to the metaphor of journeying from one point to another, there is also present in John's
thought the image of a journey into one's own depths to find
God (though this is less prominent than in St. Teresa's image of
entering ever more deeply into the "interior castle" of the soul).
This image suggests the dynamism of the Christian life as going
progressively deeper into the self in order to find union with the
God who is always present to us within, holding us in existence.
In *The Spiritual Canticle*, he writes, "It should be known that the
Word, the Son of God, together with the Father and the Holy
Spirit, is hidden by his essence and his presence in the innermost
being of the soul. Individuals who want to find him should leave
all things through affection and will, enter within themselves in
deepest recollection, and let all things be as though not" (C.1.6).
Since we are ourselves "his dwelling and his secret inner room
and hiding place," we must leave aside the superficial and seek
to join him in this inner sanctuary within ourselves (C.1.7–9).
"The soul's center is God" (F.1.12).

The Christian's itinerary, as John of the Cross sees it, can be
described as a journey from love into Love. It begins with the
discovery, in faith, of God's gratuitous love for us and invitation
to communion. Divine love awakens our love—we are wounded

---

7. St. John's sketch of the mount and description of it is reproduced in both his original
Spanish diagram and an English translation and rendering of it on pages 160–61.

by love—and we set out in hope of attaining that unimaginable gift. The final goal is nothing less than union with God—union *in* God, participating in the very life of God in the love that flows for all eternity among the three Persons of the Trinity. This amazing reality is called "divinization" or "deification" because we become God, not by nature, but by participation in the heart of the divine life: "Everything can be expressed in this statement: The soul becomes God from God through participation in him" (F.3.8). This is a window into the profoundly trinitarian nature of John's mysticism that is particularly prominent in *The Living Flame of Love*, where he writes, "The Blessed Trinity inhabits the soul by divinely illuminating its intellect with the wisdom of the Son, delighting its will in the Holy Spirit, and absorbing it powerfully and mightily in the unfathomed embrace of the Father's sweetness" (F.1.15).

But, as we have said, the path that leads to the realization of this tremendous gift of union is an ascent, a steep climb. This is not because God has chosen to make it difficult for us or to set up obstacles. The problem is in us. God loves us freely and completely, but we find ourselves unable to do either in return. Our freedom to love God is restricted by the distractions, the attachments, and the enslavements of creaturely things that are infinitely less than God. It is as if we had set out to claim the ultimate jackpot but allowed ourselves to get distracted by shiny but ultimately worthless baubles; or as if the grandest of all prizes were held out to us but we were unable to reach out for it because of the trinket in our grasp that we refused to put down; or as if our greatest hero, superstar, or idol wanted to move into our home, but we couldn't clear out the clutter to let him or her in. These analogies do not begin to approach the absurdity of the reality of living in sin and attachment. And more, such images cannot even begin to make sense to us until we have

allowed faith to open our eyes and ears to the reality of that ultimate jackpot, that prize of prizes, that superstar knocking at the
door. Many of us are so distracted that we don't even realize that
these wonders are there for us to embrace, much less have any
appreciation of their value and how we might attain them.

John uses a variety of terms to describe this sometimes difficult path or task that leads to union—purgation, purification,
emptying, darkening—but today we might call it liberation. Our
freedom must be "liberated" so that we can finally and fully accept
the divine invitation without attachment or distraction. We must
seek freedom from our attachments, our blindness and skewed
vision, from our inner disorder, and ultimately from our own selfish narcissism so that we can completely love God in response
to the divine love and invitation. Real love of any kind always
requires freedom, but it is precisely this deep freedom that we
lack. "For freedom Christ has set us free," says St. Paul (Gal 5:1).
This is the true freedom of the children of God—not a superficial
freedom to decide between this object or that, between this particular action or another, but the freedom to leave behind all that
hinders us, holds us back, and enslaves us, so that we can love God
with a freedom restored by grace, a freedom made free. This is the
gift of the saving action of Jesus Christ, and it is the path of liberation that the Doctor of Mystical Love wants to teach us. Ultimately, of course, it is God who must enable us to love the divine,
transcendent reality, though in the beginning it might feel as if we
ourselves are doing all of the heavy lifting.

Famously, in *The Ascent* and *The Dark Night*, John lays out a
four-part itinerary, corresponding to two different dimensions in
us and to two agents—ourselves and God. By doing so he wants
both to encourage us to set out and to enlighten the path that
must be trod. He speaks of these periods as different experiences
of "night." The entire liberating process is a "night" because the

work of liberation feels so difficult, because we must travel so often in the darkness of faith without seeing and understanding, and because God is infinitely beyond our capacity to grasp. God is a light so brilliant that we are blinded into darkness.

In *The Ascent*, John reflects on the two "active" nights; one is the "active night of sense," in which we work with God's help to liberate our disordered desires for objects that we can perceive through our senses. In the two subsequent parts of the same book, he focuses on the "active night of spirit" which accomplishes a deeper purification, using the divine gift of the theological virtues—faith, hope, and love. In *The Dark Night*, John teaches us about the "passive night of sense" in which God, the principal agent, draws us into a deeper contemplative prayer precisely by withdrawing our good feelings and our ability to meditate actively in prayer. John goes on to explain the "passive night of spirit," in which God works a painful but essential inner liberation of our thoughts and attachments to anything that is less than God (and, as John will insist, any concept, image, or thought about God is always infinitely less than the divine reality). Liberated at last from sin, attachment, and enslavement—and ultimately from ourselves—we are prepared to receive the divine gift of union with the triune God, the "spiritual marriage" of the soul and God.

This journey of liberation is, of course, also a journey of prayer, an ascent that depends on prayer and that deepens prayer. John of the Cross is explicitly describing and explaining the path to an ever-deepening union with God, leading to "mystical" experiences and union, experiences that are "hidden" from the normal functioning of our senses. *The Spiritual Canticle* and *The Living Flame of Love* reveal and illuminate, to the degree possible, the advanced ways and divine encounters of this path of prayer. Still, it must be said that St. Teresa is the great teacher of prayer, while John is the theologian and the teacher of the arduous steps that lead along that path made possible ultimately by divine gift. He makes clear that he does not intend to devote much attention to the life of beginners on the journey nor to the early stages of prayer. There are, he says, many published works of devotion and prayer for that purpose. In fact, books that offered meditation points, especially on the life of Christ, in order to increase devotion were plentiful in sixteenth-century Spain. (*The Spiritual Exercises* of St. Ignatius of Loyola were based on such meditations, though his work ultimately leads to a still-deeper prayer.) John has no methods to teach. His focus is on the work that we must do so that God can do that work in us by which God draws us into union with the Trinity. This is God's gracious will for us all.

A Few Tips for Reading John of the Cross

The traditional and useful advice to someone who is beginning to read St. John of the Cross for the first time is to begin with the poetry and with either *The Living Flame of Love* or *The Spiritual Canticle*. *The Ascent of Mount Carmel* focuses on the ascetical effort that is required to prepare oneself for the gift of union, while *The Dark Night* focuses on God's purifying work in this ongoing process. Many a first-time reader begins with *The Ascent*, which makes logical sense in terms of the unfolding of the spiritual life as John understands it, only to give up because of the work's Scholastic analyses and its demanding doctrine.[8] Wherever one begins, it is important to keep John's overall vision in the forefront of one's thinking and perhaps to glance

---

8. In a wonderful and sympathetic footnote to book 3 of the *Ascent*, Kavanaugh complains of the Scholastic tendency, occasionally evident in John of the Cross, to multiply distinctions and divisions: "He [John] now so multiplies subdivisions that he allows himself to enter a forest without exit." This "forest without exit" might explain the fact that *The Ascent* simply ends abruptly. *The Collected Works*, 329n1.

again from time to time at the poetry as a reminder that all of these challenges are part of a journey of love responding to Love. Even sections of John of the Cross's writing that might seem particularly dense and dry remain part of a great "science of love." Based on the context provided by this chapter, a few suggestions might be helpful for the first-time reader.

First, we must recall, as John reminds us, that he is trying to express in words—and to explain and analyze—experiences that are ultimately ineffable, unable to be captured in concepts or to be described in words. No wonder that John of the Cross, like other Christian mystics, begins with poetry that captures better the mysterious wonder of such hidden experiences of God. He is clearly possessed of a fine analytical mind, a superb theological education, and talent as a writer. But at times he seems to be vague or even confusing in what he is trying to express. This is the result of the ineffability of the experience itself.

Second, John of the Cross was a man of his time. The Scholastic philosophy and theology that he had studied gave him the framework and language to put into words profound spiritual experiences, and he has done so masterfully, producing a truly classic systematic spiritual or mystical theology. Still, none of us possesses exactly the same academic formation and manner of expression as John of the Cross—not to mention differences in temperament. He himself realizes that there might be other ways to speak of the same realities, and he was willing to draw from different theological schools of his time to find ways of understanding and explaining his experience. As readers of another time and culture, we must accept that in his writing we will find forms of analysis and expression that might not be our own. Profound and timeless truth remains within the historically bound framework that John provides, worthy of our effort to translate his ways of thinking into our own contemporary modes.

Third, every historical text must be read remembering the audience and situation to which it was originally directed. John of the Cross was writing for friars and nuns of the recently established Carmelite reform and to devout laity associated with them in sixteenth-century Spain, as described previously. Many within this original audience had become discalced Carmelites precisely because of their eagerness to embrace the eremitical and contemplative roots of Carmel. Because they were formed in this age of great spiritual and religious renewal, we can assume that his original readers were fervent and even rigorous. They had not become associated with the reform in order to find a comfortable or undemanding spiritual life. In his writing, therefore, John does not have to devote much attention to promoting devotion, defending the importance of prayer, or teaching prayer techniques to beginners. Instead, he can jump right into the heart of the issue without mitigating or softening its demands. What might seem excessive or exaggerated today would probably have been understood very differently by nuns, friars, and committed lay people eager to climb the steep but direct path that leads to the peak of Mount Carmel.

Fourth, beyond the need to recognize that he is addressing an already fervent audience, we must remain cognizant of the fact that John of the Cross is simply taking with utter seriousness the demands of the Gospel—all the references to denying oneself, taking up one's cross, selling what you have, not looking back, emptying oneself. For John, none of these Gospel phrases and injunctions was meant to be read as a pious exaggeration to make a point. John is not speaking to the halfhearted or to those willing to settle for a sincere but mediocre Christian life (A.Prol.8). In Jesus Christ, the utterly transcendent God calls and enables creatures, sinful human beings, to enter into eternal, loving union. John of the Cross wants nothing more—and nothing less—than to show us the sometimes demanding but sure and safe path to such a seemingly impossible gift. He is not trying to convince anyone either of the worthiness of this one true goal or that the trials along the way are worth the struggle; John assumes his readers already believe this.

Finally, John believes in the utter transcendence of God. He belongs to what has been called the *apophatic* tradition of Christian spirituality, with its emphasis on the God who always transcends our concepts and thoughts, and thus he emphasizes prayer that is increasingly without image, thoughts, or meditations. The path of deepening prayer is a paradoxical path of unknowing and darkness.[9] This contrasts with the so-called *kataphatic* tradition with its emphasis on images and meditations as vehicles for encounter with the God. Perhaps each of us will find a preference based on our own temperament, and so one spiritual teacher will be preferred to another. But there is no doubt, in any case, that the God whom we seek calls us, still and always in our humanity, into a sharing in God's own unfathomable nature.

For Questions for Reflection / Discussion see pages 152–153

---

9. Of course, according to John of the Cross, beyond the darkness—and even in the midst of darkness—the person encounters the true Light that is God. It is, in fact, the excess of light as God draws near that causes a spiritual blindness or darkness, just as physically a very bright light can "blind" us. Ultimately, then, beyond the negation that the term apophatic suggests, John of the Cross can be called a mystic of light or of fire, as becomes apparent in *The Living Flame of Love* and even in *The Sayings of Light and Love*. Cf. Lawrence Cunningham, "John of the Cross, Mystic of Light," *America* 194 (January 30, 2006): 22–25.

2 Love Awakened by Love: The Asceticism of the Ascent

One dark night,
fired with love's urgent longings
—ah, the sheer grace!—
I went out unseen,
my house being now all stilled.

The Dark Night, stanza 1

S t. John of the Cross was a person madly in love with God—
"fired with love's urgent longings" (N.1). And like any person head over heels in love, he saw everything that was contrary to or outside of his love for his Beloved as a waste, a hindrance, or a bother. He invites his readers to awaken to such love and to live its consequences. If we begin a reading of *The Ascent of Mount Carmel* and its companion work, *The Dark Night*, with this truth in mind, we can make sense of what might otherwise seem harsh or dry in John's doctrine. It is no surprise that first-time readers are often invited to begin with the poetry, *The Spiritual Canticle* or *The Living Flame of Love*, in which the power and depth of the saint's love is evident. On the other hand, a first-time reader of *The Ascent* who fails to understand that John of the Cross is writing about a path to attain loving union with

the Beloved or fails to keep it in mind will feel that the path offered by John is nothing but negation, drudgery, and hardship.

John of the Cross appended to the beginning of *The Ascent* a diagram of the path that leads to divine union (see pages 160 and 161). It serves as a summary and reminder of the spiritual doctrine that he had prepared for those to whom he offered guidance. The diagram, then, is also a type of summary of what will unfold in the rest of the book. Along the bottom of the diagram, we read,

> To reach satisfaction in all
> desire satisfaction in nothing.
> To come to possess all
> desire the possession of nothing.
> To arrive at being all
> desire to be nothing.
> To come to the knowledge of all
> desire the knowledge of nothing.
>
> To come to enjoy what you have not
> you must go by a way in which you enjoy not.
> To come to the knowledge you have not
> you must go by a way in which you know not.
> To come to the possession you have not
> you must go by a way in which you possess not.
> To come to be what you are not
> you must go by a way in which you are not.

Reading this text (which also appears in the body of *The Ascent* [A.1.13.11]) without knowledge or recollection that John of the Cross is concerned with teaching a way of love in response to divine love, it might seem that what he is saying is harsh and utterly world-denying. But note that in each couplet the seemingly harsh demand is preceded by the lofty goal, the unimaginable hope. We must "desire satisfaction in nothing" in order precisely so that we can attain satisfaction in all. We must "desire the possession of nothing" because we are hoping to "possess all." We must go by a path that we do not enjoy because we want to rejoice in a good that is infinitely greater than what would otherwise be attainable to us. Perhaps it is precisely because we are so often unaware or at least inattentive to the "all" that Almighty God wants to give to sinful creatures that we fail to see that so much of what we want in this life is really, ultimately "nothing." John of the Cross is showing us, straightforwardly and without apology, that we must let go of what is ultimately paltry so that we can embrace and be embraced by all that God truly wishes to give us: divine love, God's very self.

In a similar way, the diagram shows us a clear and direct path that leads to the peak of Mount Carmel, a symbol for God. Within this path, repeated seven times, is the word "nothing" (*nada*); and on either side of this straight and central path we see the words "not this . . . nor this . . . neither this" to show us that none of the various listed goods can lead us to God. This is the famous "*nada* doctrine" of John of the Cross. Again, it seems harsh, and a reader might be tempted to recoil at the seemingly negative path that John is presenting. But the important thing to see and to keep in mind is that John is laying out a straight and clear path that leads to union with Almighty God. As he will say time and again, in order to attain God, we must let go of everything that is not God or less than God. These other things, as we shall see, are not bad in themselves, but they are infinitely less than God and thus distractions for the lover who wants to move quickly, without delay, and without hindrance, to the attainment of the Beloved.

If we keep in mind that John of the Cross is called the Doctor of Mystical Love, we can see the purpose of his sometimes unapologetically hard teaching. In fact, the book begins with this preface: "This treatise explains how to reach divine union quickly. It presents instruction and doctrine valuable for beginners and proficients alike that they may learn how to unburden themselves of all earthly things, avoid spiritual obstacles, and live in that complete nakedness and freedom of spirit necessary for divine union." John is offering sound spiritual doctrine to people who are serious about their commitment. So, again without apology, John says as he draws close to the end of his prologue: "We are not writing on moral and pleasing topics addressed to the kind of spiritual people who like to approach God along sweet and satisfying paths. We are presenting a substantial and solid doctrine for all those who desire to reach this nakedness of spirit" (A.Prol.8). And, as we shall see, such "nakedness of spirit" is an utterly essential preparation for union with God in love.

God's Love Demands a Totality

Theologian Bernard Lonergan famously described religious conversion as "an other-worldly falling in love . . . a total and permanent self-surrender without conditions, qualifications, reservations . . . not as an act, but as a dynamic state."[1] This falling in love with God in its totality then takes up within itself all other spiritual and moral striving. Lonergan's definition of religious conversion describes well the reality and the demands of love as John of the Cross understood them. To love God truly involves the whole of our being in total response to God.

---

1. Bernard Lonergan, *Method in Theology* (New York: Seabury, 1972), 240.

The author of the First Letter of John tells us that our love
for God is possible only because God has first loved us: "In this
is love, not that we loved God but that he loved us and sent his
Son to be the atoning sacrifice for our sins" (1 Jn 4:10). "We love
because he first loved us" (1 Jn 4:19). God is love, and the divine
love consists in the divine self-offering, the gift of God's own
life. Love is not merely an activity or a characteristic of God.
God *is* love; and, therefore, to say that God loves is to say that
God gives the divine life itself. This is clearest to us in the gift
to humanity of God's only begotten Son, the Second Person of
the Holy Trinity. There is perhaps hardly a Gospel passage more
well known than this one: "For God so loved the world that he
gave his only Son, so that everyone who believes in him may not
perish but may have eternal life" (Jn 3.16).

For John of the Cross, God's love for us is not simply a reality in the past. God's infinite love seeks us and calls to us now, at
this moment and at every moment. John says, "In the first place
it should be known that if anyone is seeking God, the Beloved
is seeking that person much more" (F.3.28). In *The Spiritual
Canticle*, which describes the soul so enraptured with love that
it feels "wounded" with love for the Beloved (C.1.17–22), the
Beloved too is wounded with love for the soul (C.13.2). Even as
the soul seeks after him, the Bridegroom comes to seek refresh-
ment in "the spring of his bride's love" (C.13.11).

The infinite and transcendent God gives divine life. God has
given all and offers all. On the one hand, we could say that as a
result God expects all from us in return, but the requirement of
a totality of response on our part is not really so much a demand
from God. Nothing that we could give to God—even our entire
being—could even in the smallest way approach a just return or
add anything to God. We could say, on the other hand, that the
totality of our response is at least our best effort at expressing

gratitude for so amazing a gift as the divine self-gift, and that is certainly true enough. But more, God invites us into divine communion, into a mutuality in union. If we are to receive from God the gift of the divine life and respond to it, we must empty ourselves, renouncing everything that holds us back or stands in the way of our self-giving to God. And this is precisely what John of the Cross sets out to teach us when, for example, he recommends to a group of nuns who had sought his counsel, "Accordingly, those who seek satisfaction in something no longer keep themselves empty that God might fill them with his ineffable delight. And thus just as they go to God so do they return, for their hands are encumbered and cannot receive what God is giving. May God deliver us from these evil obstacles that hinder such sweet and delightful freedom" (Lt 7).

Loving God does not bring us some extrinsic reward—as if by giving myself freely to God I can now merit some recompense. Loving God is what we are made for. It is our authentic and ultimate fulfillment. One of the most fundamental beliefs about our humanity, based in the first chapter of the book of Genesis (1:26–27) is that human persons are created in the image of God, and God is love. We are created in the image of a God who *is* love, which means that love is our truest nature; love is our most authentic activity; love is our origin; and love is our destiny. We are fully who and what we were meant to be when we are loved and love in return. On the other hand, we act against own truest nature when we fail to love. We are made to love God and neighbor, so the path that John of the Cross lays out is both the path that leads to loving union with God and the path that leads to the truest fulfillment of our identity as humans. Ultimately, the divine love wants to transform us into love through participation in the very life of the Trinity (2 Pt 1:4).

In his *Summa Theologiae*, St. Thomas Aquinas teaches us that love is the "form" of the virtues (II–II, q.23, ad.8). Love directs all of our virtues and actions to God. In that sense, love forms in us a complete response of our entire being to God's love. Our love for God, when made effective in our lives, empowers, shapes, and unites all of our desiring, choosing, and acting into our self-giving to the triune God. As the Letter to the Colossians challenges us, "Above all, clothe yourselves with love, which binds everything together in perfect harmony" (Col 3:14). Commenting on the line "now my every act is love" in the twenty-eighth stanza of *The Spiritual Canticle*, John of the Cross says of the advanced soul, "All the ability of my soul and body (memory, intellect, and will, interior and exterior senses, appetites of the sensory and spiritual parts) move in love and because of love. Everything I do I do with love, and everything I suffer I suffer with the delight of love" (C.28.8).

To read his works is to see how the spirituality of John of the Cross fits into a tradition of Christian mysticism called "love mysticism."

Taking Jesus at His Word

John's language and images of absolute surrender to God and the demands of loving God can strike some readers as excessive. In fact, John of the Cross is simply taking Jesus at his word as it appears in the Gospels:

> Jesus says that we must deny ourselves, take up our cross, and lose our very lives (Mt 16:24–28; Mk 8:34–9:1; Lk 9:23–24).

> We must go and sell everything we have and give to the poor (Mt 19:21; Mk 10:21; Lk 18:22).

> We must let the dead bury their dead and not look back (Mt 8:21–22; Lk 9:59–62).

Anyone who loves father and mother more than Christ is not worthy of him (Mt 10:37); or if one does not hate father and mother or even one's own life, that person cannot be his disciple (Lk 14:26).

If our eye causes us to sin, we should tear it out (Mt 18:9).

We are invited to enter through the narrow gate that leads to life rather than follow the wide road that leads to destruction (Mt 7:13–14; Lk 13:24).

The texts could be multiplied. Even accounting for some hyperbole, Jesus calls for the response of one's entire being. In fact, Jesus makes his own the command from the book of Deuteronomy (6:5) that demands that we love God totally—with heart, soul, and strength (Mt 22:37–40; Mk 12:28–31; Lk 10:25–28).

John of the Cross draws his demanding doctrine not only from the explicit teaching of Jesus but also from the Savior's example. The self-giving of God in the incarnation and the redemptive action of the Son, and especially the example of Jesus totally surrendered and emptied on the cross, is the heart of the lesson that John wants to teach us. This is nothing more than the teaching of St. Paul in the powerful Philippians hymn (2:5–11) in which he challenges us to take on the mind of Christ Jesus who "emptied" and "humbled" himself to the point of giving his life on the cross. As goes the master, so must go the disciples. This is a hard message. No wonder that, having just dramatically professed Jesus as Messiah, Peter rebukes Jesus nonetheless for predicting the passion. The implications of the impending suffering and death of the master are not lost on his chief disciple. Jesus rebukes Peter in return and then goes on to lay out the implications quite explicitly: "If any want to become my followers, let them deny themselves and take up their cross and follow me" (Mk 8:27–38;

Mt 16:21–27; Lk 9:18–27). As the master goes, so must the disciples follow.

Perhaps today we have become so accustomed to these hard sayings of Jesus and the Gospel vignettes that we don't think much about them. Or perhaps we interpret the sayings as purely homiletic exaggeration to make a point. Maybe we could tell ourselves that all of the talk of self-denial and taking up the cross has some pious, secondary meaning restricted to certain "spiritual" aspects of our lives. What is clear is that John of the Cross takes the sayings and the stories with complete seriousness, and he does so not simply because they express some extrinsic command of Jesus. Rather, they express the logical unfolding of what it means to love an infinite God who has first loved us and called us to share in the divine life.

Part of our difficulty in seeing these biblical demands with the same seriousness that John of the Cross did is that we do not ponder enough the totality of God's gift to us and the totality of Jesus' surrender on the cross out of love for us. Maybe we have not entered deeply enough into the Good News of God's love for sinners and the divine invitation to share in the divine life itself and what this means and demands. It is certainly true that we read the Scriptures today more critically than Christians did in the time of John of the Cross, and it is true that the emphases of our spirituality are different in a time and culture far distant from sixteenth-century Spain. But what cannot be denied is that there is no salvation without the cross. There is no Christian discipleship that does not embrace the cross in its many forms, whether in suffering that cannot be avoided or in the challenge of trying to live the Christian life authentically. Is John of the Cross mistaken in finding in the message and example of Jesus the fundamental truth that real Christian discipleship admits of no mediocrity or compromise?

If we wish to soften or tone down the demands of Jesus, then the demanding teaching of John of the Cross too would need to be taken with a grain of salt. But if Jesus means what he says as the Scriptures record it, and if he intends for his example to provide a lesson for his disciples of every age and culture, then John is really not saying anything that the Savior himself did not already say with equal force and bluntness.

Attachments Stand in the Way

All of the teachings about purgation from John of the Cross are about freeing ourselves so that we can love God in return and enter into the union to which we are invited. All of the obstacles to complete love of God and divine union are from our side: distractions, attachments to things, enslavement to our desires. Even if we sincerely desire to respond to the divine self-offer, we find ourselves burdened by the effects of sin. We must, as John says, be purified, emptied, and liberated from everything that holds us back.

We do not see the world aright. Often we do not measure the always relative value of its good things as we ought. The world around us is the good creation of a good God, but it remains infinitely less than God. The good things that can be attained or acquired in this world can be good, pleasing, and satisfying. But we are blind if we think that anything at all that is created can approach, even in the smallest way, the goodness of God and God's power to fulfill, please, and satisfy our deepest needs and longing. In comparison with God, the good things of earth are like the tawdriest of imitations. Putting it starkly, John of the Cross tells us, "All the beauty of creatures compared to the infinite beauty of God is the height of ugliness. . . . All the grace and elegance of creatures compared to God's grace is utter

coarseness and crudity. . . . Compared to the infinite goodness of God, all the goodness of the creatures of the world can be
called wickedness. . . . All of the world's wisdom and human
ability compared to the infinite wisdom of God is pure and
utter ignorance" (A.1.4.4). As St. Paul reminds us in a similar
way, "The wisdom of this world is foolishness with God" (1 Cor
3:19). With eyes that see more clearly than many of us do, Paul
also tells us that he counts all else as "loss" and "rubbish" in comparison with the value of knowing Christ and the promise of
attaining life with him (Phil 3:8).

In book 1 of *The Ascent of Mount Carmel*, John of the Cross
teaches us about what he calls the active night of sense. With the
help of grace, the work of purification in this early stage is the
result of our active efforts. We experience it, he says, as a type of
night because we are depriving ourselves of our accustomed plea-
sures. It feels like a kind of darkness. Later this purifying work
will go deeper and require that God become the principal agent,
but here at the beginning what is operating is our graced effort
to purify ourselves specifically of our attachment to sensory,
material goods.

John of the Cross explains in several ways why we cannot
remain attached to earthly things and truly love God. These are
not typical ways of thinking in our day, yet they still reveal deep
insight into our human loving and our limitation.

Jesus teaches in the Gospels, "No one can serve two mas-
ters; for a slave will either hate the one and love the other, or
be devoted to the one and despise the other. You cannot serve
God and wealth" (Mt 6:24; see also Lk 16:13). John of the
Cross intends to offer a similar lesson in telling us, following the
thought of Aristotle and Aquinas, that "two contraries cannot
coexist in the same subject." He says, "Since love of God and
attachment to creatures are contraries, they cannot coexist in the

same will" (A.1.6.1). Perhaps we see this most clearly in a more extreme—though sadly not uncommon—example of someone who has no time, energy, or focus for God in a life driven by an appetite for success, pleasure, wealth, human respect. In the end, in order to enter into communion with God, we must create an emptiness within ourselves so that nothing distracts us or serves as an obstacle. "This uncreated fullness [which is God] cannot enter a soul until this other hunger caused by the desires is expelled" (A.1.6.3).

Another line of thought (which might strike us as odd) is the classical philosophical idea that "love effects a likeness between the lover and the thing loved." He means that when we love something, it enters into us through our desiring and pursuit of it, and we subordinate ourselves to its attainment. In a similar way, the Catholic moral tradition teaches us that our actions do not simply exist outside of ourselves. By choosing to do certain things and act in certain ways, not only do we create some action or product outside ourselves, but also by the very act of choosing an action, we make it part of ourselves. I cannot intentionally harm another person and think that my action exists only outside myself. No, by the very act of choosing, I have made myself into a person who harms other people. The bad intention, the malice, exists in me. In a similar way, by loving someone or something as a conscious activity rather than simply as a passing and superficial emotion, I take that person or thing into myself in a mysterious way. I make myself into a lover of that person or thing, for good or ill. So John teaches us that love "effects a likeness," even an equality, between the lover and the loved: "Anyone who loves a creature, then, is as low as that creature and in some way lower because love not only equates but even subjects the lover to the loved creature" (A.1.4.3). Rather than loving God and thus raising ourselves to God by divine grace, we choose to love mere creatures and end up being, in that sense, lower than ourselves: "Love causes equality and likeness and even brings the lover lower than the loved object" (A.1.4.4).

When we think about the fact that loving effects a likeness to the thing loved, it is all the more amazing that God loves us, sinful creatures. This divine love and its effect are most clear in the incarnation. The transcendent and infinite God becomes lower in loving us and, more wonderful still, raises us up by baptism into the paschal mystery so that we, mere creatures, can love God in return.[2]

In our age, without denying John's other insights, it may be better to repeat his teaching that unruly appetites for mere things and attachment to them are a distraction from our true purpose. And more, they can enslave us, preventing us from making the choices that we ought. (Think of how easy it is, for example, to neglect prayer because we have so many other "important things" to do.)

In speaking of the necessity of a total purification of our sensory appetites, John notes, "It makes little difference whether a bird is tied by a thin thread or by a cord. Even if it is tied by thread, the bird will be held bound just as surely as if it were tied by a cord, that is, it will be impeded from flying as long as it does not break the thread" (A.1.11.4). Thus, it is not enough to free ourselves of mortal sin or serious attachments. John says that we must overcome even our venial sins and conscious, voluntary imperfections (A.1.11.2). It must be noted that John is not saying that we are capable in this life of eliminating every imperfection, nor is he saying that the problem is our desires in themselves. We are, after all, merely human, and desire is part

---

2. Kieran Kavanaugh, O.C.D., highlights this truth in *The Collected Works of St. John of the Cross*, trans. Kieran Kavanaugh, O.C.D., and Otilio Rodriguez, O.C.D., rev. ed. (Washington, D.C.: ICS Publications, 1999), 124n2.

of human nature. Again, as we have seen, the problem is in our will—in choosing to act on, give in to, and become a slave of our unruly appetites and remain intentionally content with a range of "little" imperfections. Many of us would probably be pretty content to eliminate serious sin, and the avoidance of venial sin would be icing on the cake. But John's message holds true: God offers all and wants to take possession of us in love, but we can be neither truly empty ourselves nor able to respond fully if we are attached even to small things that are not God.

The Problem of Asceticism Today

John's message on the need to empty and purify ourselves to attain union with God is not likely to appeal to many people today, formed as we are by a "me"-focused culture that insists on more and more, and immediately. The whole idea of asceticism (from a Greek word meaning "struggle") is not even in the vocabulary or thought world of many contemporary Christians. An overemphasis on misguided ideas of the past can explain part of the contemporary loss of a sense of values like self-denial, asceticism, and purgation. The word "asceticism" itself might for some conjure up images of gaunt, emaciated monks or fanatics scourging themselves with whips to quiet their unruly sexual passions.

We live in a culture that is little given to the idea of voluntary struggle. It has been said that we live in an age of "entitlement"—some people feel that they are entitled to good things without having to work for them. We are a society of instant gratification, of ever-new inventions to make things easier for us, of "easy come, easy go." How can the traditional value of sacrifice and purification in the spiritual life find a place in the lives of even sincere Christians formed in our culture?

Certainly, contemporary Christian spirituality is more world-affirming and incarnational, one that embraces our embodiment. Our emphasis has shifted from God as a stern judge or demanding father to a God of love. God is love, like the father of the Gospel's prodigal son. All of these developments are good and reflect a return to biblical sources for our spirituality. At the same time, formed by our broader culture, perhaps we do suffer from an attitude of spiritual entitlement. For many Christians, the God who is love has become a kind of doting, forgetful grandfather who makes no demands, who accepts whatever we do, and who will erase the consequences even of our own decisions. To say that the path to God requires effort and struggle seems like a denial that God is love. An indulgent grandparent, after all, would never ask of us anything harsh or difficult.

No one believes in a God who is love more than does St. John of the Cross. No one is filled with more wonder at the divine love for sinful creatures. John of the Cross's image of God is not a harsh judge who demands hardship and struggle in order to attain the union that God holds out to us. But, at the same time, John of the Cross takes with utter seriousness the deeper meaning of love and the demands of that love. Every human being who has ever really loved another person knows that true love is not a passing feeling without commitment. Real human loving is not just an emotional state; it is an act of the will, a daily renewed commitment. It requires fighting a spirit of selfishness. It requires sacrifice. Real human loving is a struggle. Ask any married couple serious about their commitment. The struggle to free ourselves is not based on some arbitrary demand imposed by God from outside of us. It is the inner necessity that we discover in ourselves as soon as we realize that loving God as we want is hard, requiring sacrifice, self-denial, and purification. It is precisely the commitment and the daily effort to love on ordinary days, day in and day out, that purifies us, with God's help, over time.

What Purgation Is Not

Having reflected on the hard work of purgation in this active night of sense, it might be useful to say explicitly what purgation is not. Our list is not exhaustive but suggestive of the positive meaning and value of purgation.

First, the necessity of purgation does not imply that either the created order or the good things of this earthly life are evil in themselves. The problem arises because we allow these things to distract, obstruct, or enslave us. John says explicitly, "Since the things of the world cannot enter the soul, they are not in themselves an encumbrance or harm to it; rather, it is the will and appetite dwelling within that cause the damage when set on these things" (A.1.3.4). The problem is that we sometimes choose these things instead of God—even though they are infinitely less than God and only bear the tiniest trace of God's goodness. John of the Cross, as his contemporaries report, was a great lover of both natural beauty and music. As he says in the fifth stanza of *The Spiritual Canticle*, the created things of this world are marked by the beauty of their Creator: "having looked at them, / with his image alone, / clothed them in beauty."

Second, the need to purify our desires is not based on any sense that these desires are evil in themselves. To be human is to desire. The problem is that we desire what we should not, desire it more than God, or allow our desires to rule us or to enslave us. John of the Cross was a man of great passion for God. His spirituality, as his poetry shows, is highly affective. Desire is not the enemy, nor is the body in which such desire resides. Our embodiment too is part of our nature, the result of a good creation, taken up by God in the incarnation and redeemed in Jesus Christ. The body is not the problem, nor the desires that reside in it.

Third, the authentic work of purgation should not leave us dour and restricted. Again, John's contemporaries describe him as a man of great joy, warmth, and good humor. His letters reveal that he loved others and was loved in return. Purgation is a liberating work that enables us truly to love others and to appreciate the true beauty of people and things without selfishness and self-serving interests.

Fourth, purgation is not anti-pleasure. Pleasure is simply the enjoyment we experience in possessing a good. God has made us in such a way that what is authentically good should give us pleasure. Experiencing it is meant by God to serve both as an encouragement to seek the good and as a reward for attaining it. The problem is taking pleasure in what is not good for us or pleasure as a superficial end in itself, which only promotes selfishness and distracts us from the true and worthy.

Despite the fact that the purifying work of this active night of sense is difficult at times, the effort is directed at making us more truly human and more capable of receiving God's love and of giving love in return. The good news is that ultimately having truly tasted of divine love and goodness, the soul comes to lose its taste for merely created things for their own sakes (C.10).

Entering into the Active Night of Sense

So we must set out along the sometimes arduous path to ascend Mount Carmel—the path that seeks the attainment of loving union with the God who is love. Since John's purpose is to help us along this way, he concludes his teaching about this active night of sense by offering practical advice for entering into this work of purification (A.1.13). He tells us that we must develop the habitual desire to imitate Christ and to live in conformity to him. This requires that we study and meditate on his life, teachings, and example. Secondly, we must actively renounce our tendency to find merely superficial satisfaction, to seek the easiest path, to please ourselves. As is often the case, he elaborates on this path in a way that, on first reading, can strike the modern reader as harsh:

> Endeavor to be inclined always:
>
> not to the easiest, but to the most difficult;
>
> not to the most delightful, but to the most distasteful;
>
> not to the most gratifying, but to the less pleasant;
>
> not to what means rest for you, but to hard work;
>
> not to the consoling, but to the unconsoling;
>
> not to the most, but to the least;
>
> not to the highest and most precious, but to the lowest and most despised;
>
> not to wanting something, but to wanting nothing.
>
> Do not go about looking for the best of temporal things, but for the worst, and, for Christ, desire to enter into complete nakedness, emptiness, and poverty in everything in the world. (A.1.13.6)

It must be noticed that he says "endeavor to be inclined." He is talking about an attitude or disposition of the mind rather than giving directions for each and every action. Further, he immediately says that we should put this counsel into practice "with order and discretion" (A.1.13.7). In any case, I think that we can understand the meaning of his advice by drawing a parallel to an athlete who must have a determined attitude and resolve and who must then enter into a repetitive discipline that requires practice at many levels in activities and skills that are not necessarily the same as the precise skills essential to the sport. It has been traditional in Christian spirituality to say that at times we can combat a particularly entrenched vice by denying ourselves in another area. For example, in order to overcome lust, it can sometimes be helpful to fast. We are, after all, a unity. Our will is one, and discipline applied in one area of our life can yield fruit in another.

More positively, John urges us to enkindle a different desire and longing, beyond our desire and attachment to material and superficial things. We must nurture a new and different love. In so doing, we will find new power to turn away from our misguided and disordered desiring:

> A love of pleasure, and attachment to it, usually fires the will toward the enjoyment of things that give pleasure. A more intense enkindling of another, better love (love of the soul's Bridegroom) is necessary for the vanquishing of the appetites and the denial of this pleasure. By finding satisfaction and strength in this love, it will have the courage and constancy to readily deny all other appetites. . . . For the sensory appetites are moved and attracted toward sensory objects with such cravings that if the spiritual part of the soul is not fired with other, more urgent longings for spiritual things, the soul will be able neither to overcome the yoke of nature nor to enter the night of sense; nor will it have the courage to live in the darkness of all things by denying its appetites for them. (A.1.14.2)

In the end, the important virtue for us on this path is perseverance, more than fervor. St. Teresa of Avila called it a *"muy determinada determinación"* (a very determined determination).

We must persevere in our effort, with God's help, to know God's love for us more deeply, to empty and free ourselves so that we can love in return, and to love each and every day in ways both great and small.

John of the Cross is a man madly in love with God, and he wants to awaken us to God's love and guide us on the path to union with God. Beyond our imaginings and ability, God has loved us, and awareness of God's love awakens love in us. We must nurture that love for God—at first, an affective love that increases devotion, and then a deeper spiritual love that longs for nothing other than, and nothing less than, loving union with God.

He who is sick with love,
whom God himself has touched,
finds his tastes so changed
that they fall away
like a fevered man's
who loathes any food he sees
and desires I-don't-know-what
which is so gladly found.[3]

For Questions for Reflection / Discussion see pages 153–154

---

3. Stanza three of "A gloss (with a spiritual meaning)," in *The Collected Works*, 71.

3 The Theological Virtues

In order to journey to God the intellect must be per-
fected in the darkness of faith, the memory in the
emptiness of hope, and the will in the nakedness and
absence of every affection. (A.2.6.1)

T he theological virtues of faith, hope, and love play a central
role in the thought of St. John of the Cross. Perhaps no other
classical spiritual teacher in the Christian tradition has emphasized their decisive role in the process of sanctification as much
as John.[1] In *The Ascent of Mount Carmel*, John focuses most distinctively on the purifying role of the three theological virtues
on the path to union with God—faith darkening the intellect,
hope emptying the memory, and love liberating the will. John
of the Cross did not set out to write a treatise on virtues, and he
presupposes some understanding of concepts that are not always
emphasized in contemporary spirituality. In order to recognize
the valuable insight that he offers us, it will be useful to look
more broadly at virtues in general and more particularly at the
theological virtues and how they have traditionally been understood to function in the Christian life. His unique insights will
then become even more evident.

---

1. Eulogio Pacho, *San Juan de la Cruz: Temas Fundamentales II*, Colección Karmel 17 (Burgos, Spain: Editorial Monte Carmelo, 1984), 98.

Virtues and Vices: A Primer

Contemporary Christian ethics has rediscovered the central place of the virtues. Catholic and Protestant theologians alike draw on the classic teaching of St. Thomas Aquinas and certain strains of contemporary philosophical ethics to see the essential role of virtues and vices in the Christian life.[2] The good Christian life is not just about good actions performed and bad actions avoided but also about our abiding attitudes, our priorities and values, and our view of ourselves in relationship with God, other persons, and the world around us. Aquinas's moral theology is essentially centered on virtues. Although this focus was largely lost for centuries in Catholic moral theology, it was retained before the Second Vatican Council in manuals of spirituality (or, as it was called, ascetical and mystical theology).[3] In a particular way, these older manuals devoted attention to the role of the theological virtues, often drawing in some way on the thought of the Mystical Doctor.

Classically and systematically presented by St. Thomas Aquinas, moral virtues are, simply put, habitual dispositions to do the good.[4] They are abiding tendencies, most often formed over

---

2. For a good example of a recent introduction to Catholic moral theology that views the moral life principally through the lens of the virtues, see William C. Mattison III, *Introducing Moral Theology: True Happiness and the Virtues* (Grand Rapids, Mich.: Brazos Press, 2008). For a more foundational introduction to what has come to be called "virtue ethics," see Joseph J. Kotva Jr., *The Christian Case for Virtue Ethics* (Washington, D.C.: Georgetown University Press, 1996).

3. One of the last such manuals, drawing together insights from earlier such works, is Jordan Aumann, O.P., *Spiritual Theology* (London: Sheed and Ward, 1980).

4. A good introduction to Aquinas's discussion of virtues in general, as well as the theological and cardinal virtues, is provided by the chapters in Stephen J. Pope, ed., *The Ethics of Aquinas* (Washington, D.C.: Georgetown University Press, 2002). For a classic discussion of the cardinal virtues, see Josef Pieper, *The Four Cardinal Virtues* (Notre Dame, Ind.: University of Notre Dame Press, 1980), a collection of essays on prudence, justice, fortitude, and temperance, originally published separately in the 1950s. Similarly, Pieper's *Faith, Hope and Love* (San Francisco: Ignatius Press, 1997) is a collection of essays that appeared separately over a period of more than thirty years.

time through our efforts aided by grace. Once established, they make it easier for us to do the good without struggle and effort even when the temptation to act otherwise is great. For example, we build up the virtue of honesty by telling the truth in one situation after another, by resisting the temptation to lie or to color the truth, and by repenting and resolving to do better after each fall. At first, perhaps with difficulty and inconsistency, but gradually with greater ease and facility, we build up the virtue until it becomes almost second nature. We are then truly honest people—people who tell the truth not just occasionally, from time to time, but consistently, habitually, and without struggle. We have acquired, always with the help of grace, the virtue of honesty. For Aquinas, all the moral virtues are in some way related to the cardinal virtues of prudence, justice, fortitude, and temperance.

There are, tragically, bad habits as well, which we call vices. These too are built up over time by decisions. Each time we fail to resist a temptation or repent of an evil and each time we choose an evil, we build up a vice such as dishonesty or at least weaken a virtue that we had previously established with some firmness.

Aquinas taught that the natural moral virtues are "acquired," which is to say that we ourselves develop these good habits, with the help of grace, by our choices and actions over time. In addition to these acquired virtues, St. Thomas taught that there are also "infused" virtues—that is, good habitual dispositions that God gives us in order to open us to divine assistance in our moral living. They come to everyone who lives in grace ("sanctifying grace," as it is traditionally called). For each natural, acquired moral virtue, there is a parallel infused moral virtue by which God further empowers us to the good. The theological virtues of faith, hope, and love are a particular type of infused virtues that direct us beyond this merely human life, with its immediate goal of becoming authentically good human persons, to become saints, which God calls all of us to be. As gifts, the infused virtues must be gratefully received; while as virtues, they must be embraced, nurtured by repeated choice, and acted upon.

The theological training of John of the Cross, as we have said, was eclectic, though foundationally Augustinian, in keeping with the Carmelite theology of his time. Still, without suggesting that John was a Thomist, Aquinas's teaching on virtue and vice would have been well known to John because it plays such a prominent role in St. Thomas's discussion of the moral life.[5] John has no particular reason to offer to his readers a treatise on virtues. He simply presupposed that after the sincere Christian overcomes the temptation to commit individual acts of serious sin, the task moves deeper: to overcoming vices and growing in virtues. Sinful acts are rooted in vices, while good actions are rooted in virtues. Uprooting vice and fostering virtues require conscious and committed effort, and much grace. The working of grace to aid our moral striving and the infusion of virtues represent God's assistance in our moral efforts.

John of the Cross provides no treatise on virtues, except for his lengthy and distinctive discussion of the theological virtues, which is the focus of further chapters of this work. He would most likely explain that there are many fine books that deal with this topic. At the same time, he gives witness in a number of key places to the importance of growth in virtue—especially in infused moral virtues—as well as attending to the contrary reality of vice. Early in his discussion of the passive night of sense

---

5. John of the Cross does not take up the breadth of St. Thomas's teaching on infused virtues and the relationship, in particular, of the theological virtues and the gifts of the Holy Spirit. Fuller discussion of the role of the gifts of the Holy Spirit in the Christian life developed after his time. See Federico Ruiz Salvador, *Introducción a San Juan de la Cruz: El hombre, los escritos, el sistema* (Madrid: Biblioteca de Autores Cristianos, 1968), 448–49.

in *The Dark Night*, he provides a relatively lengthy discussion of the capital vices, conceived as spiritual imperfections that God must overcome through the divine action at work in us. (We will examine his teaching on these vices in a later chapter.) In the prologue of *The Spiritual Canticle*, before commencing his commentary on the first stanza of the poem, John begins with a glance at the entire Christian journey (C. Introduction, Theme) but quickly focuses on its more advanced stages, frequently referring to the virtues broadly but importantly. Those who truly seek God must take up "the practice and works of the virtues," which are described as mountains to be climbed and heights to be attained (C.3.3–4). God "breathes into the soul" the virtues in order to renew and move these dispositions so that they can become apparent as they are needed, like the buds of flowers waiting to open or like aromatic spices that release their scent when uncovered (C.17.5). The virtues are like "dens of lions" that come to protect the soul from moral and spiritual harm: "Thus when the soul possesses the perfect virtues, each of them is like a den of lions in which Christ, the Bridegroom, united with the soul in that virtue and in each of the others, dwells and assists like a strong lion. And the soul herself, united with him in these same virtues, is also like a strong lion because she thereby receives the properties of God" (C.24.4). The virtues brought together in love, like a bouquet of flowers, give delight to the soul and to God (C.16.7–9). In fact, together, they are like a garland of flowers that adorns the soul and gives joy to the soul and to God together (C.30.2–8).

The Theological Virtues

Faith, hope, and love are infused virtues. They are described as "infused" because they are given by God and not "acquired" by our own effort. At the same time, they are virtues—which is to say that they are abiding habits, dispositions for acting—which, once received as a gift, can be strengthened or weakened, embraced or ignored, acted upon or lost. They inhere within us; they become part of who we are and how we act in the world. More particularly, they are "theological" virtues because they are directed immediately to God and enable us to cooperate with God's action, drawing us into the divine life. Natural moral virtues aim at natural human goodness or integrity—becoming a truly good human person. The theological virtues direct us to union with God, which is the only true and ultimate fulfillment of our humanity.

God is infinitely beyond us. We cannot attain divine communion by any action or natural human capacity. Only God can reach across the infinite divide that separates the transcendent God and creation to draw us into union. We cannot know God truly by the unaided use of our intellects; mere creatures and sinners besides, we cannot hope for communion with a transcendent God by anything we can accomplish; we cannot possibly love God as God deserves. God must reach down, so to speak, to make possible what is impossible for us on our own. This is the work of the theological virtues.[6] By the gift of faith, we can come to believe and truly to know God as God is. By hope, we can trust and even expect that God will make possible the fulfillment of our desire to respond to the divine invitation to communion. With the theological virtue of love, we can love God with the love with which God fills us. In grace,

---

6. In addition to the works on virtue cited above, see also Josef Ratzinger (Pope Benedict XVI), *To Look on Christ: Exercises in Faith, Hope and Love* (New York: Crossroad, 1991); Romanus Cessario, O.P., *The Virtues, or the Examined Life* (New York: Continuum, 2002); and, from a contemporary Protestant perspective that draws as well from traditional Catholic sources, see Elaine A. Robinson, *These Three: The Theological Virtues of Faith, Hope, and Love* (Eugene, Ore.: Wipf and Stock, 2004).

God gives us the divine presence of the Holy Spirit as well as the means to respond to the divine self-offer and to the call to yet deeper union.[7]

In a fundamental way, the gift of the theological virtues makes it possible for us to become truly and fully human. We are made to know, to love, and to long for a transcendent God, but we cannot do so completely unless God gives us the capacity to do so. Without the theological virtues, we cannot become what we are meant to be. Perhaps this truth becomes most obvious in the absence of these great virtues, whether through serious sin or simply through a lack of attention and effort to nurture them. Our world, the result of God's good creation, is graced in so many ways. Yet we humans who inhabit it often lack faith and belief. It can be no surprise then that it often also lacks the authentic vision, hope, and challenge that are the fruit of faith. In a world where so many are in need, at so many levels, alongside examples of generous service, we see the unwillingness and perhaps the inability to rise to a selfless love for others. Too often, when people long for the possibility of hope and an invitation to dream for better, they are met by and seemingly forced at times into cynicism and despair.[8]

In the theological virtues we see the amazing love of God that invites and then empowers sinful creatures into a communion that is infinitely beyond their own capacity to attain. St. Thomas offers us a wonderful parallel to God's action in giving us the theological virtues when he speaks of charity as friendship with God.[9] Following Aristotle, Aquinas presupposed that there can only be true friendships between equals. A king cannot be a friend with a slave or a noblewoman with her servant.

7. Ruiz, *Introducción a San Juan de la Cruz*, 455.

8. Robinson, *These Three*, 48–49.

9. *Summa Theologiae*, II–II, q.23, a.1.

But it is simply impossible for there to be equality between God and human beings. How then, asks Aquinas, can there be friendship? What is impossible from our side, God makes possible by bridging the infinite divide between us. God comes down to us and raises us up to the divine. This is the incredible mystery of the incarnation in which God became human, divinity taking on created human flesh. God came down to our human, creaturely level; and through our baptism into the saving death and resurrection of the incarnate Son of God, we are raised up. By God's action and gift, then, human persons can realize the impossible: they can enter into friendship with God. As St. John of the Cross says, "With God, to love the soul is to put her somehow within himself and make her his equal" (C.32.6). Through the gift of the three theological virtues, we are given the necessary means to embrace this divine friendship as well as a share in it already in this life.

The incarnation was a divine mystery that most fascinated John of the Cross. That the infinite and transcendent God invites us into divine communion and makes it possible—because only God could do so—is a reality that continually fills him with wonder. United with Christ, even in this life, we are invited to participate in the very life of the Trinity: God loving God within us, our participation in the eternal relationship of love within the life of God. This is the transforming union, and it is built on the gift of the theological virtues by which God empowers us to accept the divine invitation. God must invite us into union; then God must provide the means and does so primarily through the theological virtues.

Faith, hope, and love are God's gift to those who remain open to the divine presence and action; they are habits, abiding dispositions. We can see, then, as John of the Cross will emphasize, that we must take up the gift, embrace it, and put it to work in order to accomplish God's purpose for giving us the gift. In fact, these virtues are both divine gift and further empowerment for our own human effort. It becomes our task to cooperate with God's action and put these divinely given dispositions to work. We must continually dispose ourselves to live according to faith, hope, and love.[10] For John the same theological virtues that aim to unite us with God do so precisely by purifying us at the deepest level.

Traditionally, the Christian life lived in harmony with the working of the theological virtues in us has been called the "theological life." It is a life directed toward God, enlivened with the divine life and action, in which our thoughts and actions are in conformity with the loving will and purposes of God. This is the challenge of John of the Cross to us in books 2 and 3 of *The Ascent*: to live the theological life fully as it opens out in the divine life itself.

Faith, Hope, and Love Together

The three theological virtues are given together as a gift, and they work together in uniting us with God.[11] They can be distinguished, and as John will emphasize, their differing functions can be identified. But together they are the working of God in the one whole human person who is open to the divine self-communication.[12] The growth of each one of these virtues

---

10. José Damian Gaitan, *Negación y plenitud en San Juan de la Cruz* (Madrid: Editorial de Espiritualidad, 1995), 243–47.

11. John of the Cross suggests (A.2.6.5) that the three theological virtues can be seen in the Gospel parable (Luke 11) in which one friend comes to another at midnight to ask for three loaves. The loaves represent these three virtues, and the fact that they are requested at midnight represents the fact they must be acquired in this night of the spirit.

12. Ruiz, *Introducción a San Juan de la Cruz*, 444.

brings the growth of the other two (A.2.24.8; A.3.1.1). The development of one of them alone would be drastically incomplete without the others (A.3.16.1).

Aquinas had taught that, although the three virtues are given together, we can say that faith must be first because we must know the end (which is communion with God) before we can strive for it in hope or embrace it in love. Faith in God gives birth to the hope of attaining so amazing a goal, and it awakens love for the God who, in faith, we have come to believe has so loved us. But looked at another way, Aquinas says, love precedes faith and hope because these other two are formed by love and reach their perfection in love.[13]

Moral theologian Bernard Häring suggests that the three theological virtues are three different aspects of our fundamental life commitment—our "yes" to God. In faith, we say "yes" to God in belief and in trust. In hope, we say "yes" to the future that has been offered and promised. In love, we say "yes" to God's loving self-offer. God extends the divine self-offer and then empowers us through these three theological virtues working together to embrace it.[14]

The Distinctive View of John of the Cross

John of the Cross discusses the important role of the theological virtues in what he calls the active night *of spirit*.[15] The dedicated Christian has largely ordered his or her desires and affections, overcome serious sin, and grown in virtue. This was the work

---

13. *Summa Theologiae*, I–II, q.62, a.4.

14. Bernard Häring, C.Ss.R. *Timely and Untimely Virtues* (Middlegreen, England: St. Paul Publications, 1986), 33–41.

15. John addresses the theological virtues together especially in chapter 6 of book 2 of the *Ascent*.

of the active night *of sense* described in book 1 of *The Ascent*. It was "active" because the principal agent is the person, acting in cooperation with God's grace; it was "sense" because the focus of the purification is our attachment to, or enslavement by, objects available to our natural senses. The second stanza of the poem *The Dark Night*, which serves as the launching point for John's discussion of the theological virtues, ends with the line "my house being now all stilled." The active night of sense has brought order and calm to the previously disordered affections so that the person of prayer is now ready to engage, with God's help, in a deeper work of purification. On the one hand, it is a great good fortune to have arrived at this new stage. On the other hand, as John says, there is a "greater hardship involved in quieting the house that is one's spiritual nature" (A.2.1.1)

In John's spiritual itinerary, the active working of faith, hope, and love coincides with the introduction of the gift of contemplation (A.2.6.8; A.2.7.13). After a long period of discursive meditation—prayer with images and reflection—and with one's house now "being all stilled," God draws the person away from active prayer into the more passive or receptive prayer of contemplation. This transition is the passive night of sense in which God withdraws feelings, consolations, and felt experiences of the divine presence in prayer. The person is left in dryness but still with a deeper longing for God.

God's gift of contemplation—for such prayer can only be a divine gift—comes at the same time in which the gift of the theological virtues begin in earnest their work of emptying the person of all that is not God. In contemplation, God gives the divine presence—at first, a passing but real experience of union with God. Hand in hand with this tentative encounter and making growth in contemplative prayer possible, God cleanses the person through the theological virtues of all that is less than

God: "Faith causes darkness and a void of understanding in the intellect, hope begets an emptiness of possessions in the memory, and charity produces the nakedness and emptiness of affection and joy in all that is not God" (A.2.6.2). "Consequently, these three virtues place a soul in darkness and emptiness in respect to all things" (A.2.6.4). Contemplative prayer grows in just such darkness, emptiness, and nakedness.

John of the Cross distinctively and creatively links each of the three theological virtues with one of the three basic human faculties that he identifies: faith with the intellect, hope with the memory, and love with the will.[16] In doing so, John follows the Augustinian distinction of three human faculties or powers (intellect, memory, and will) rather than the twofold Thomistic distinction (which would become more dominant in the subsequent history of Catholic theology) of the two faculties of intellect and will. Again, John shows the eclectic nature of his academic training and his willingness to draw elements from different schools of thought. In the end, it is not clear if John was drawing from a firmly held, personal, more comprehensive anthropology in which these three faculties have their respective functions or if the tri-part division simply served his purposes in explaining the action of the theological virtues. In any case, John's reliance on three faculties enables him to unfold rich insights on this deeper work of preparation for ever-deeper and more prolonged union.

Theoretically, within the active night of spirit we can distinguish the purifying tasks of the theological virtues in this way: faith brings darkness to the intellect; hope brings emptiness to

---

16. It would certainly be possible to offer a critique of Scholastic faculty psychology with its division of human powers or capacities into intellect, will, and memory, but for our purposes we will simply accept the divisions that John is using and try to draw contemporary insight from them.

the memory; and love brings nakedness to the will. At the same time, while we can say that faith works in the intellect, really it impacts the person at multiple levels and in many ways. So too with the other theological virtues. Furthermore, we can say that just as the intellect, memory, and will are different powers of a human person who is essentially one, so too the experience of darkness, emptiness, and nakedness are fundamentally different aspects of a profound purification of anything that is not God. In sum, we can say again that the theological virtues and their particular roles in the work of purification can be distinguished but not really separated.[17]

Although he focuses his attention on the purifying role of the theological virtues in *The Ascent*, John of the Cross sees at the same time that they are also unifying. Faith, hope, and love direct us to and unite us with God. This becomes clearer in *The Dark Night* when John presents the theological virtues together as a kind of vesture that disguises the person from the enemy and that serves as a nuptial garment appropriate for the celebration of the spiritual marriage of the soul with God. Faith is an inner tunic of white; hope, a green coat of mail; and love, a red toga (N.2.21). These three virtues together empty the person of all that is not God and, at the same time, remodel, perfect, and dispose the person to live the Gospel and enter more completely into communion with God.[18] John says, "Because these virtues have the function of withdrawing the soul from all that is less than God, they consequently have the mission of joining it with God" (N.2.21.11).

In fact, the theological virtues are not just some form of extrinsic assistance, merely a means to union with God. To some

---

17. Ruiz, *Introducción a San Juan de la Cruz*, 451–52.

18. Gaitan, *Negación y plenitud*, 242.

degree they represent in this life that full union we are striving to attain. Faith is already an obscure knowing of God present to us; hope is already God's presence in our desiring; and God is at the heart of all of our loving. These virtues already unite us to God in the measure that we live them. To live them perfectly would be to be perfectly united with God: "Only faith, hope, and charity (according to the intellect, memory, and will) can unite the soul with God in this life" (A.2.6.1).[19]

In reflecting on divine union in *The Living Flame of Love*, John speaks of these faculties of intellect, memory, and will as "deep caverns" (F.3.17–22): "They are as deep as the boundless goods of which they are capable since anything less than the infinite fails to fill them" (F.3.18). But it is not until they are "emptied of, purged, cleansed of every affection for creatures" that we can experience their infinite depth. As human beings, we are made for union with a transcendent God, amazingly created as an infinite capacity for an infinite God (F.3.22). Cleansed by the gift and the work of the theological virtues, the intellect will no longer understand naturally but by union with the divine intellect; the will shall not just love creatures, imperfectly, but rather love them united with the divine loving; the memory will no longer be limited to images that have their base in created things but will open out to an infinite horizon (F.2.34).

Let us turn now to an examination of each of the theological virtues.

For Questions for Reflection / Discussion see page 154

---

19. Ibid., 239–40n15.

4 Faith

"This book is a treatise on faith, the proximate means of ascent to union with God." This is the heading with which St. John of the Cross opens book 2 of *The Ascent of Mount Carmel*. The second major part of *The Ascent* begins as a commentary on the second stanza of his mystical poem *The Dark Night*, which he quotes at the beginning of chapter 1:

> In darkness and secure,
>
> by the secret ladder, disguised,
>
> —ah, the sheer grace!—
>
> in darkness and concealment,
>
> my house being now all stilled. (N.2)

Faith is this "secret ladder" by which we ascend to God in darkness—that is, without knowledge that comes through the natural senses and that could be expressed in concepts and beliefs about God. True, mature faith is a dark faith. There is no natural ladder, physical or intellectual, that can possibly lead us to God. We need to walk a dark path by which God alone can lead us (A.2.8.7).

The theological virtue of faith plays a central role in the thought of John of the Cross. He devotes all of this second book to it, while discussing hope and love more briefly together in book 3. For him, faith purifies the intellect in preparation for union with God. In order to understand how this is so, we must provide a broader understanding of faith in general and in the thought of John of the Cross in particular.

Natural Faith

In fact, every human person lives, to some degree, by faith. This is obviously not to say that everyone has Christian faith, believing in the Good News of Jesus Christ and the doctrines taught by the church. Rather, everyone lives by a kind of natural faith in the sense that we all believe in realities that we do not actually see.[1] Understanding faith in this general sense can help us to understand the nature of explicit Christian faith.

It is a common human experience to believe that we know things of which we personally have no empirical evidence or experience. I can say, for example, that there is a planet that we call Neptune that circles our sun. I would say that I know it as a fact. But I have no personal evidence or experience of it. I have never been to Neptune, never seen it even through a telescope, and have never met anyone who has been there. Rather, my knowing is based on a kind of natural faith—that is, faith in the testimony, knowledge, and reliability of others. In fact, many, perhaps most, of the things that I believe that I know about science, geography, or history depend on such a faith. Of course, in many of these cases, empirical evidence could be produced, but we can see at least that faith itself is fundamentally a kind of knowing that is not based on empirical evidence.

This natural faith extends beyond mere facts. A young father standing in a backyard pool says to his little daughter on the pool's edge, "Jump and I'll catch you." Well, the little girl has no empirical evidence that her father will, in fact, catch her—or even really attempt it—but nonetheless she "knows" that he will. Why? How does she know it? By a kind of faith. She has faith in her father. She knows that she can trust him, rely on his word

---

1. See Josef Pieper, *Faith, Hope and Love* (San Francisco: Ignatius Press, 1997), 19–54.

and his care, without proof in this moment and this situation. Yes, we can say that he has given evidence of his trustworthiness and his parental concern in the past. But, at this moment, the little girl will step out in faith.

Christian Faith

Clearly, Christian faith too is a kind of knowing that is not based on immediate empirical evidence. We believe in God, what is revealed about God in the Bible, and what is taught about God by the church without being able to prove any of it, at least according to any scientific method. True, the central point of our faith is a real flesh-and-blood, historical human being, Jesus of Nazareth. But the truth of what he taught and revealed is accepted by faith. Still, if we have such faith, we know what we believe to be true. And the deeper our faith, the deeper our assurance of its truth.

In the end, Christian faith, unlike the facts that we accept with a natural faith, cannot be verified empirically. Christian faith is not principally about facts at all. It is rather a vision of reality, of what is truly real and valuable. In faith we accept as true not just particular doctrines. Rather, we believe that what God has revealed, most especially in the teaching and life of Jesus Christ, constitutes the truth of our entire existence. We not only come to believe doctrines *about* God; we also come to believe *in* God, in a way akin to the little girl who has faith in her father. Christian faith is not just beliefs or knowledge *about* God; it is faith *in* God; and ultimately, as John of the Cross will insist, it is a loving knowledge *of* God.

Christian faith is a gift. Since it is not based fundamentally on empirical evidence, we must be invited and empowered to come to see with eyes of faith the reality that it reveals. We cannot make ourselves believe. We cannot simply reason our-selves into it. Even if it might feel that we had arrived at faith on our own, it is in fact always a gift of God's grace.

Christian faith is a gift, but it is a gift that must be embraced. The gift can be offered and refused. It can be accepted but squandered. It can also be sidelined, ignored, and left to wither. God offers the gift of faith, but we must accept that gift. Perhaps this is not so apparent in the case of children who are simply raised in the faith from infancy, but even in those cases eventually each person will have to decide, as an adult, to embrace and live his or her faith. And in the face of the challenges to our faith presented by such contemporary temptations as materialism and consumerism, by widespread indifference to religion, and by sin, both individual and social, our faith must be not only a decision but also a commitment—and a commitment that is regularly, even daily, renewed. In this sense, the gift of faith can grow and deepen.

Christian faith is a gift; it is a decision and commitment as well as a virtue. As John of the Cross says, "Faith, the theologians say, is a certain and obscure habit of soul. It is an obscure habit because it brings us to believe divinely revealed truths that tran-scend every natural light and infinitely exceed all human under-standing" (A.2.3.1). Christian faith is a habit in the sense that it does not come and go. To the degree that it is authentic, we don't turn it off and on. If we have the virtue of faith, we see God, other people, the world, and ourselves in an abiding way. When we come to new situations or circumstances, we come already disposed to see and to value in particular ways.

Like all the virtues, including the theological virtues, faith must be embraced. The virtue of faith must be strengthened. It must be made more secure against other incomplete or false ways of seeing and knowing.

Faith as Communal

In contemporary discussions of Christian faith, we would view any such reflection as incomplete without some focus on faith as communal or ecclesial. Faith is always passed on, formed, nurtured, and celebrated within the context of the Christian community. We do not believe alone. The gift of faith, while truly personal, unites the Christian to a body of believers who together celebrate a God who invites them into community in this life and in the life to come.

John of the Cross does not give much attention to this aspect of faith. Of course, he did not set out to write a systematic theological treatise on faith. Still, John's desire to submit his teaching to the official teachers of the church and its commonly held doctrine implies faith's communal nature. Nor was John writing a comprehensive presentation of the Christian life. He simply presupposed that his readers, as committed Christians actively seeking union with God, would be involved in the sacramental life of the church. He was clearly grateful for the faith that he had received and in which he had been raised in the heart of his deeply Christian family, and his religious life was profoundly communal as well. In the end, it was evident to him that the deeply personal journey of the Christian into the heart of the triune life of God would reveal clearly his or her communion with all others in God.

Faith in an Utterly Transcendent God

When we think about faith, we might immediately think of the beliefs and doctrines that the church teaches about God and about God's relationship to humanity. This is certainly an essential element of faith. Growing up in the Christian community and learning about Christian faith, we must learn the church's basic beliefs, especially as these are present in the Creed that we recite each Sunday at Mass. Through these beliefs that constitute the Christian faith, we come to some knowledge of who God is and how God interacts with us—knowledge that is reliable because it has been divinely revealed and faithfully handed on and taught by the church.

Knowing about God moves us to love God all the more. Of God it can truly be said, "To know God is to love God." The more we know God, the more we must love God. Faith reveals that God is love, as well as the Good News that this God loves sinners; and the deeper our faith in this truth, the more we must love in return. The more we love, the more we want to know—until we come to the realization that our loving must surpass our ability to know God, at least according to our usual way of knowing. The God who loves us and whom we love in response is a God who is completely beyond our ability to know as we know other things in this life.

John of the Cross explicitly embraced the Christian faith in the sense of doctrines and beliefs, and trusting in it, he unhesitatingly placed his teaching under the scrutiny and judgment of the church's doctrines and official teachers (A.Prol.2). He rejected any idea that what might seem to be revealed to an individual could override what had been divinely revealed in the Scriptures and handed down by the church. The doctrines of our faith are sure and reliable, and they offer us some measure of certain knowledge about God.

At the same time, John insists on the utter transcendence of God. God is ultimately and always beyond us. We will never be able to grasp this infinite God fully, certainly not in this life, nor even in the next. God is transcendent, and it is precisely this reality that makes the divine invitation to mere humans to enter into communion all the more incredible. The impossible is made possible because the infinite God who is love wills it and makes it possible.

The reality of an infinite and transcendent God simply cannot be contained by anything that our minds can grasp. If we could do so, this knowable "God" would not really be God at all. John says, "However impressive may be one's knowledge or experience of God, that knowledge or experience will have no resemblance to God and amount to very little" (A.2.4.3). God remains always Mystery, and we cannot—and we should not try to—reduce the divine to what the natural human intellect can grasp on its own. In the end, this is the contemplative path, beyond concepts and images about God, a path drawing us instead into the ineffable mystery that is God.

Faith as adherence to doctrines and beliefs has an important place in the Christian life, especially for those who are beginners on the Christian path. Belief is the necessary foundation or boundary that can keep us from going astray, but these doctrines cannot be thought to capture the truth of who God is. We must not confuse these doctrines with God as God is. We are invited into a true encounter and union with God. Christian doctrines and theological ideas can serve an important purpose on this journey; but just as God is beyond our ability to understand in any normal way of knowing, our journey leads us beyond the knowledge of God that these doctrines can contain. Invited into contemplative knowledge of God, as John says, "all that can be grasped by the intellect would serve as obstacle rather than as a means if a person were to become attached to it" (A.2.8.1).

Dark Faith Purifies the Intellect

John of the Cross is inviting us into a more mature faith that is not attached to what we can know about God, no matter how sublime. The Christian must want God as God truly is—not simply knowledge about God and certainly not knowledge that, in the end, must be infinitely less than who God truly is. The faith that John invites us to embrace is a dark faith, a faith that does not see or know God in any merely human way. It is a faith that is necessarily darkness to the natural intellect, our usual way of knowing.

It is in this sense that faith must purify the intellect as we travel the path to deep union with God. Since God cannot be contained by what our intellect can know and since even doctrines about God fall so infinitely short of the divine reality, in order to truly know God, we must put aside any attachment to what our intellect can attain on its own.

In part, this darkening effect of mature faith is the result of our own effort in response to God's invitation and help. This is, according to John, the *active* night of spirit. We must actively free ourselves of attachment to any concepts about God and any inclination to think that we have truly grasped God through such knowing. Without such active purification, we will simply be unable to surrender to the deeper knowing of God that is never the result of any action of our human intellect.

At the same time, such dark faith is God's gift to the Christian who has already begun the work of letting go of all that is less than God. Recall again that the active night of spirit occurs as the person is invited by God into contemplative prayer, beyond images and concepts and beyond active meditation. Rather, dark faith is itself an encounter with God, and, as an encounter with the transcendent God, it causes darkness in the intellect that is not prepared for the encounter. Paradoxically, dark faith is the divine light but experienced as darkness. As John says, just as a brilliant light will overpower a lesser light and just as a bright light will blind us, so too the drawing near of God darkens the intellect (A.2.3.1). We will say more about this in the sections that follow.

The Reality of Dark Faith in Our Experience

If we return for a moment to our earlier reflection on natural faith, we can get a glimpse of what St. John of the Cross means by this dark faith. When a man and woman choose to marry, even after a long relationship, there is always an element of mystery. Is this really the person for me? Will he or she remain faithful? Will I later meet another person who seems better suited to my dreams? In the end, the couple will choose to make a lifetime commitment that is not based on empirical evidence. Yes, over time they have given one another reason to trust, but at the moment of commitment there is a kind of blind or dark faith in the other. There is a knowing that is beyond the evidence already presented, a knowing that is not based on new ways of proving the cause for their believing.

In this sense, we see too how faith is a way of knowing that is born of love. The bride and groom know each other and they know the other's trustworthiness with a knowledge born of love. Love in this sense is a way of knowing. The dark faith of the Christian too is a way of knowing born of love—a knowledge that does not involve facts or evidence but that is no less sure and reliable. Such faith is born of our acceptance of the truth that God has first loved us in Christ, but it is a faith that love has led us into, a faith that passes beyond dependence on what can be known about our Beloved. A contemplative knowledge of God is a connatural knowing—a deeper knowing that comes, not from observing and thinking, but by our participation in love in the life of God, certainly imperfectly in this life, but that we hope is always deepening. Faith is leading us to a knowledge of God not with concepts or feelings but in love. It is for this reason that Aquinas teaches that charity is linked with the gift of wisdom because the person of deep charity can discern God's will by an intuitive insight.[2]

In our common way of speaking, when we say that someone has "stepped out in faith," we mean that the person has made a decision without knowing with certainty how it will turn out. St. Peter literally stepped out in faith when, in the storm on the Sea of Galilee, he stepped out of the relative safety of the wave-tossed boat to walk to Jesus on the water (Mt 14:22–33). This too is an analogy to the dark faith of which John of the Cross speaks. It is a faith without knowing, beyond evidence, and beyond the need to prove and to attain certainty. An equally dramatic biblical example of such faith is the story of the sacrifice of Isaac (Gen 22:1–19). Abraham is commanded by God to sacrifice his long-awaited and precious son, Isaac. He sets out to follow this command, believing that somehow God has a plan, a way out, an unexpected good yet to be discerned. In short, Abraham sets out in dark faith (see Heb 11:17).

Perhaps our ability to understand what dark faith is and what it requires is rooted in the experience of a suffering that cannot be eliminated, ignored, or escaped. Illness, tragedy, failure, death, and many other such difficulties are an inevitable part of every human life. Having Christian faith and being a person of prayer does not exempt us from this reality. In the midst of such situations it is natural enough to wonder where God is, why God doesn't intervene, and to ask the question that so often has no response in this life: "Why?" Christian faith does not bring immunity from these human realities, but it invites us to believe and to trust that God is nonetheless present. In fact,

---

2. *Summa Theologiae* II–II, q.45, a.3.

true Christian faith requires it. We might not see, feel, or experience God, but we believe with a kind of dark faith that God is present. God is invisibly at work, to bring out unimagined good from tragic evil, as God did when Jesus rose triumphant from the apparent defeat of the cross. This is, as John of the Cross tells us, the dark faith of Jesus on the cross (A.2.7.9–11). In this light, St. Paul says, "We know that all things work together for good for those who love God" (Rom 8:28). In other words, God is at work in the midst of even the most unlikely and painful situations to bring unexpected good for those who love. This we know in faith.

A kind of dark faith can see us through the unavoidable challenges of our lives. At the same time, living through life's difficulties, clinging to a faith that does not experience God in the moment, opens us to a more authentic encounter with the living God. We come to a truer knowledge of God who is now that much less the child's naive vision of a God who fixes every problem and makes life easier for good people. Such a dark faith is a more mature faith. A Christian faith that has walked through the experience of suffering comes out as a more authentic, mature faith.

Dark Faith and Contemplative Knowing

This dark faith, this obscure knowing, is the necessary foundation for contemplation. In fact, for John of the Cross, faith and contemplation are virtually synonymous.[3] Contemplation is a wordless, imageless prayer into which God invites the Christian who has devoted himself or herself for a prolonged time to

---

3. *The Collected Works of St. John of the Cross*, trans. Kieran Kavanaugh, O.C.D., and Otilio Rodriguez, O.C.D., rev. ed. (Washington, D.C.: ICS Publications, 1999), 173n3.

discursive prayer. Contemplation, as John says, is precisely a general, loving knowledge of God.

In this active night of spirit, God has begun to invite the person of prayer into this silent, wordless praying. This development necessarily goes hand in hand with letting go of previously useful concepts, images, and even experiences of God. As authentic as they might have been, they are necessarily less than God. We must want God and not even the best concepts *about* God; God wants us to know God and not simply know *about* God.

John of the Cross talks about this according to the theological framework of his time. Following Aquinas, he accepts that all normal knowing comes through the senses (A.1.3.3). Everything that we know in a normal sense we have learned from empirical evidence—from actually seeing something or at least hearing about it or reading about it. From what we have learned from the senses, we can construct in our minds further concepts, ideas, and images. But the basis of all of this is rooted in the physical senses.

Our usual knowledge of God fits into this framework. We know about God through analogies, concepts, and images that draw on our normal senses. We say that God is like a parent, a judge, or a friend. As the psalms tell us, God is a rock, a fortress, a shield. With such images we understand something of how God is in relation to us. When we say that God creates or saves, we understand an important reality through analogies to ordinary acts of creating and saving, even if our doctrinal formulations are much more sophisticated and dense.

Of course, while we can know something of God through this way of knowing, obviously an infinite and transcendent God cannot be contained by any such knowing. As John of the Cross, and the church with him, affirms, anything we can say or know about

God is more *unlike* God than it is really *like* God. This is not to deny the truth of our doctrines, concepts, and images, nor to deny their importance and value; it is simply to say that God is beyond what we can know through our everyday channels of knowing. Faith, in its normal connotation of acceptance of a set of beliefs, involves knowledge of this kind. Such doctrines are essential in the life of Christians and of the church as long as we do not confuse them for God, think that we have even come close to grasping God through them, or become attached to them.

Dark faith is a different way of knowing, a way of knowing that surpasses our natural ways of knowing. True knowledge of God must necessarily be so. We see, then, why this dark faith must be a gift. Usually God chooses to reveal the divine reality to a person who has already done the preparation of eliminating from his or her life the grosser distractions and entanglements with mere created things.

The key point to the purifying role of dark faith acting on the intellect is that our usual ways of knowing God, through doctrines and images, can only get in the way of this true encounter and knowledge of God. How can we let go and surrender to the revelation of God in this gifted encounter if we are distracted by and clinging to ways of knowing that are, ultimately and unavoidably, infinitely less than God? How can we know God as God wants to be known, in the divine reality itself, if we remain focused on what is so much less than God? Our normal way of knowing, in this sense, is not wrong; it is just radically incomplete. It is not proven false but surpassed or transcended as God gives the gift of a more obscure loving knowledge, which is contemplation. While God can give such a gift at any moment, at any stage on the journey, it is most usually given to those who have allowed dark faith to open up a space for this deeper contemplative knowing.

At the same time, doctrines about God as revealed in Scripture, handed down in tradition, and taught by the church serve as a continuing check against the possibility of being led astray by some sincere but false personal revelation. Again, this is why John of the Cross explicitly places all of his teaching under the judgment of the church's official teachers.

Dark Faith Is an Encounter with God

In dark faith, there is a true encounter with God. Although he speaks of faith as a means to an encounter with God, at the same time for John of the Cross, dark faith is itself a communication of the divine presence. It is not only a deeper opening to the mystery of God; dark faith is itself a contemplative, loving knowledge of God who is truly present to the Christian. Faith of this kind is an encounter with the transcendent God, beyond our normal ways of knowing.[4] In *The Spiritual Canticle*, John tells us, "Faith, consequently, gives and communicates God himself to us but covered with the silver of faith. Yet it does not for this reason fail to give him to us truly. Were someone to give us a gold vase plated with silver, we would not fail to receive a gold vase merely because of its being silver-plated" (C.12.4). In *The Ascent*, he says, "Only by means of faith, in divine light exceeding all understanding, does God manifest himself to the soul. The greater one's faith the closer is one's union with God" (A.2.9.1). Further, the Son of God, he tells us, "communicates himself to the soul in faith" (A.2.29.6).

4. Ross Collings, O.C.D., *John of the Cross*, Way of the Mystics 10 (Collegeville, Minn.: Liturgical/Michael Glazier, 1990), 118. See also Federico Ruiz Salvador, *Místico y maestro: San Juan de la Cruz* (Madrid: Editorial de Espiritualidad, 2006), 245–61; and Aniano Alvarez-Suárez, "Fe teologal," in *Diccionario de San Juan de la Cruz*, ed. Eulogio Pacho (Burgos, Spain: Monte Carmelo, 2009), 461.

God wants us to know the divine reality, but it cannot be known or encompassed by our natural intellect. In the gift of contemplation God communicates this reality to the person directly, and the person's natural capacities are overwhelmed. God illumines the person with the divine presence, but since the human person lacks the natural faculties capable of grasping or even recognizing this ultimately transcendent reality, the divine illumination is experienced as darkness. God makes the divine reality known directly to the person, but it is a knowing that, because it so transcends our natural ways of knowing, is experienced as a kind of *un*knowing.[5] As John tells us, "The light of faith in its abundance suppresses and overwhelms that of the intellect. For the intellect, by its own power, extends only to natural knowledge, though it is has the potency to be raised to a supernatural act whenever our Lord wishes" (A.2.3.1).

Paradoxically, the darkness of faith reveals the deeper reality of a divine illumination: "Faith, manifestly, is a dark night for souls, but in this way it gives them light. The more darkness it brings on them, the more light it sheds. For by blinding, it illumines them" (A.2.3.4). John captures this great paradox as he recalls the classic mystical teaching of the sixth-century Syrian monk Pseudo-Dionysius: "Contemplation, consequently, by which the intellect has a higher knowledge of God, is called mystical theology, meaning the secret wisdom of God. For this wisdom is secret to the very intellect that receives it. St. Dionysius on this account refers to contemplation as a ray of darkness" (A.2.8.6). It is like the person whose natural sight is blinded by a sudden bright light or like a much brighter light that will totally encompass a dimmer light (A.2.3.1).

---

5. Mystical knowledge of God as a kind of unknowing is classically expressed in the anonymous fourteenth-century work *The Cloud of Unknowing*, ed. James Walsh, S.J., Classics of Western Spirituality (New York: Paulist, 1981).

Just as the gift of contemplation challenges the person of prayer to let God take him or her beyond active, discursive meditation, the gift of faith requires the person to embrace and to walk in this darkness of the intellect concerning any knowledge of God. "Like the blind, they must lean on dark faith, accept it for their guide and light, and rest on nothing of what they understand, taste, feel, or imagine" (A.2.4.2).

The chapter in which John begins the focused discussion of the purifying role of the theological virtue of faith is titled "Faith is the proximate and proportionate means to the intellect for the attainment of the divine union of love" (A.2.9). Beliefs about and images of God can serve only as a remote means to union with God. They can set us on the right path and keep us from straying from it, but because they cannot truly encompass God and cannot serve in themselves as a true encounter by which God is communicated, they cannot be an immediate and direct path. The Christian must be prepared to embrace and even welcome the darkness of a deeper reality of authentic faith.

The Challenge of a Dark Faith

The second half of the Mystical Doctor's reflection on faith in book 2 (chapters 10–32) of *The Ascent* is a sometimes confusing and seemingly esoteric discussion of different forms of mystical knowledge of God. While John of the Cross believes, as Aquinas had taught, that all natural knowing comes through the senses (and our subsequent reflection on and imagining about what comes from the senses), he tells us that there are other, supernatural ways of knowing, some quite sublime (A.2.10). God can reveal the divine reality by other means, bypassing our usual seeing and hearing. Most probably, such ways of knowing are not common to many of us, but it is clear that mystics and contemplatives throughout Christian history—recognized saints as well as many more men and women forgotten by human history—have received special revelations, seen visions that were not apparent to normal sight, received a "word" that was not heard with the ears, or have been filled with a profound knowledge of God even though they had never opened a theological textbook. In the book of her *Life*, St. Teresa of Avila recounts many such experiences, and John of the Cross explicitly refers his readers to the writings of "the blessed Teresa of Jesus, our Mother" for a more detailed description of such phenomena (C.13.7).

John of the Cross provides his readers with simple, consistent advice about any and all such ways of experiencing and knowing God: since experiences of God are not God and since they are infinitely less than God, no matter how sublime, they must be left behind (see, for example, A.2.11.5–6; 2.16.10; 2.17.7). There is no point, he cautions us, in devoting too much time trying to determine if a special experience or knowledge is from God, from the devil, or a figment of our own imagination. Of course, if it is from the devil or from ourselves, only harm can come from going over the experience again and again, trying to figure it out or determine its origin. If it is from God, then God has accomplished the divine intention just by providing it, at the moment God knows it is right for us to receive it. It will accomplish—or has already accomplished—what God intended; there is no need to give it further thought. In fact, it would be positively harmful to allow it to puff us up with pride, make us think of ourselves as special, or tempt us to sit back because we have "arrived." In any case, the experience or knowledge is not God in the divine totality; it is still infinitely less than God, so we must move on and continue to walk in dark faith—in the loving, obscure knowing of God, which is contemplation.

What is the "take home" message for Christians who have no experience of such special encounters with or manifestations of God? Is John's discussion here too exotic or esoteric for most of us, perhaps better edited out or at least passed over by the contemporary reader? Not at all. Reflection on what John is saying reveals that he has a profound message here for all of us. Certainly, there are many Catholics today who are fascinated by and even eagerly seeking out apparitions. They want to know the special message they believe God has for us, often through the Blessed Virgin.[6] There are Christians who are fascinated by predictions and signs, revealed by apparitions or by interpretations of the New Testament book of Revelation, of the definite unfolding of the last days. They want to read about visions of purgatory and hell or the stories of those who have died, "seen the light," and returned to tell about it. Many Christians think that their interpretation of Scripture, their image of God, or their clear apprehension of traditional doctrine about God has given them some sort of definitive and final word about God with which to cast judgment on the interpretations, images, and understanding of other Christians. And don't all of us, at one time or another, tell God, "Just tell me. Just show me. Give me a sign. Give me something"?

Surely, almost all of us would like certainty about God in a sometimes very uncertain world. We want clarity about this God on whom we are staking our lives, to whom we are giving our time, and for whom we trust that we are working in our ministries and vocations as married people, parents, religious, Christians living the single life, or priests. We want some clear knowledge of this God whom we believe is drawing close to us,

---

6. John is not addressing apparitions that are given for the good of others in the church and approved by the church. He is focusing, rather, on private revelations and experiences.

even though we know that the same God is ultimately transcendent. Often we want some "proof" for our faith, some evidence to affirm our believing. Yes, we sometimes ask for signs, but in our better moments we know that such a request reveals a weak faith. Still, rather than a crass "natural" sign, wouldn't it be wonderful to have some supernatural sign: some revelation, some vision, some profound experience?

All of this seeking after assurance is natural enough. In fact, it is profoundly human. The problem is that the profoundly human on its own cannot encompass God. In the face of our natural tendency to seek clarity, reassurance, and evidence, John urges us simply to live in faith: "In all our necessities, trials, difficulties, no better or safer aid exists for us than prayer and hope that God will provide for us by the means he desires" (A.2.21.5).

To us and to all of his readers through these five centuries, John of the Cross simply invites us again and again to walk in dark faith—that is, in a true faith in a transcendent God. God has already spoken the one definitive Word that we need: Jesus Christ. In his life, teaching, example, death, and resurrection, God is revealed to us. What more does God need to reveal? What greater evidence or more certain proof could there be? Imagining a conversation between God and a person seeking the reassurance of some special experience, John says,

> God could answer as follows: If I have already told you all things in my Word, my Son, and if I have no other word, what answer or revelation can I now make that would surpass this? Fasten your eyes on him alone because in him I have spoken and revealed all and in him you will discover even more than you ask for and desire. You are making appeal for locutions and revelations that are incomplete, but if you turn your eyes to him you will find them complete. For he is my entire

locution and response, vision and revelation, which I have already spoken, answered, manifested, and revealed to you by giving him to you as a brother, companion, master, ransom, and reward. . . . If you desire me to declare some secret truths or events to you, fix your eyes only on him and you will discern hidden in him the most secret mysteries, and wisdom, and wonders of God. (A.2.22.5, 6)

The church that is guided by the Spirit of God faithfully passes on this profound divine truth of Jesus Christ, preaching and teaching it in every age and culture, providing assurance to Christians that they are walking on the right path. The Sacred Scriptures and the sure doctrine of the church are reliable guides for our Christian living. And yet—but still—to the degree that the profound divine truth that is God revealed in Jesus Christ is formulated in human concepts, conveyed by human words, pictured in human images, limited by human ways of knowing, it is less than God—infinitely less than God.

Jesus Christ himself is the Way, the Truth, and the Life (Jn 14:6; see A.2.7.8). United with him in baptism, following him in faithful discipleship, meditating on his life and teaching, communing with him in prayer, we are led by Christ into the life of the triune God (see A.2.7.8–11). But this way is ultimately not a path of knowing more clearly and abundantly about Jesus Christ and what he reveals about God, nor embracing still more vivid and accurate images of him, nor promoting ever-deeper feelings that assure us of his presence. All of that is essential, if incomplete. The way is Jesus Christ in himself and union with him—not knowledge about him, not images of him, not feelings for him. Jesus Christ is the bridegroom of *The Spiritual Canticle* who wounds, entices, and beckons, who longs for union with us far more than we long for him. To enter his embrace, we must leave behind the beautiful flowers in the field and the messengers that he has sent, and we must walk with him in dark faith—in loving and obscure knowledge—until he leads us into the triune life and we are made one with God in him. Meanwhile, it is Christ himself who walks with us in the night.

John of the Cross has sometimes been criticized for how little he talks about Jesus Christ in his writing. He seems to say, in the interpretation of some, that Jesus must be transcended in order for us to enter into union with the triune God, but such an interpretation would be profoundly mistaken.[7] Yes, all active meditation on the life of Jesus, which is valuable at one stage of the Christian life, must be surpassed. In fact, John is addressing those who have prayed in this way for years and are anxious—and are being invited by God—to a far deeper relationship. Yes, all that we think we know about God through the revelation of Jesus Christ—the doctrines, the images, and the ways of knowing—must be transcended, not because they are not true, but because the Way, the Truth, and the Life wants us to enter into the reality that could never be fully contained by our understanding of the revelation that is Jesus Christ:

> There is much to fathom in Christ, for he is like an abundant mine with many recesses of treasures, so that however deep individuals may go they never reach the end or bottom, but rather in every recess find new veins with new riches everywhere. . . .

---

7. *The Collected Works*, 186n2. For fuller discussions of the place of Jesus Christ in John's thought, see also Iain Matthew, *The Impact of God: Soundings from St. John of the Cross* (London: Hodder and Stoughton, 1995), 114–33; Regis Jordan, O.C.D., "Jesus Christ in the Writings of John of the Cross," in *John of the Cross*, Carmelite Studies 6 (Washington, D.C.: ICS Publications, 1992), 98–108; Norbert Cummins, O.C.D., *Freedom to Rejoice: Understanding St. John of the Cross* (London: Harper Collins, 1991), 25–30.

The soul, then, earnestly longs to enter these caverns of Christ in order to be absorbed, transformed, and wholly inebriated in the love of the wisdom of these mysteries, and hide herself in the bosom of the Beloved. (C.37.4, 5)

Faith and Beyond

The theological virtue of faith is a gift, and it is an "obscure habit." It is not a single moment of insight but an abiding way of relating to God and to our knowledge of the divine. The gift of faith must be embraced. Each time that we are tempted to think that we have arrived at some way of knowing God fully or adequately through our normal understanding, we must burst our own bubble (or, perhaps even more commonly, allow it to be burst by some movement of divine grace). Every time we realize that we depend on some particular image of God, we must acknowledge its inadequacy. We cannot attain union with God if we are content to remain attached to any such image or concept.

Developing healthy images of God and overcoming prevalent images that are clearly inadequate (for example, passing from a predominant image of God as a stern and demanding judge to God as loving parent or faithful friend) are important moments in the maturing Christian life. The opportunity to study theology and to enter into the theological richness of the Christian tradition is a great privilege. But the endpoint of correcting images of God and of advancing in theological studies is not the arrival at a still better image of God nor a clearer intellectual, academic knowledge of God. Both, in the end, are woefully inadequate. Still, the gift of faith is a habit, a virtue that must be embraced over time, purifying the intellect not only by God's grace but also by our choices.

To walk in the darkness of faith, to consent to and to cooperate with its purifying power, requires abiding attitudes of trust, docility, and humility. God is at work in us. In the divine self-giving love, God wants union with us more than we ourselves could possibly desire it. We must be content with the darkness and the unknowing and, at the same time, remain open to the divine encounter that is experienced as night.

Faith, as we shall see in the next chapter, is given with the theological virtue of hope. All three theological virtues are linked. The beginnings of true faith are in the acceptance of the Good News that God has first loved sinners, and our love is awakened by this news of the divine love. It is desire for the fulfillment of love's longing that propels us forward in the path to union with God, as the fundamental images of John's mystical poetry make clear. To walk along this path in dark faith is made possible by hope in God's loving desire for union with us and by trust that God will not lead us astray nor deny us the means to attain the divine union to which we are invited.

Even in this life, at least in the final stages of union, dark faith gives way to a true, if incomplete, knowing. United with God and participating in the divine life, we will no longer know God through analogies to created things that are available to our senses; rather, it will be the reverse: we will know the created order through God's eyes—we will know not God through creation but creation through God.

For Questions for Reflection / Discussion see pages 155–156

5 Hope

> I went out seeking love,
> and with unfaltering hope
> I flew so high, so high,
> that I overtook the prey.
>
> (Stanzas given a spiritual meaning)[1]

As we have seen, the theological virtues together play a central role in the spiritual itinerary as described by St. John of the Cross. Particularly distinctive is his reflection on the purifying role of the virtue of hope.[2] He sets up an intriguing and ultimately fruitful paradox: hope (which looks to the future) purifies the memory (which looks to the past). Hope keeps our gaze set on what lies always beyond—to the One who calls to us intimately and insistently but who, in this life, remains always beyond our reach, beckoning and guiding us into divine union.

---

1. *The Collected Works of St. John of the Cross*, trans. Kieran Kavanaugh, O.C.D., and Otilio Rodriguez, O.C.D., rev. ed. (Washington, D.C.: ICS Publications, 1999), 56.

2. Certainly, the connection between memory and hope is a distinctive contribution of St. John of the Cross. The need to cleanse the memory, however, in the development of the spiritual life is taught by other classic spiritual authors. The anonymous author of the fourteenth-century classic *The Cloud of Unknowing*, for example, teaches that all created things must be placed behind a "cloud of forgetting" in order for us to advance in deep prayer. *The Cloud of Unknowing*, ed. James Walsh, S.J., Classics of Western Spirituality (New York: Paulist, 1981).

John's focused discussion of the theological virtue of hope in *The Ascent* is really more explicitly about the memory upon which hope must act. He devotes most of his attention to the obstacles that the memory presents to the attainment of union with God rather than to an analysis of the virtue of hope. A theological analysis of any of the theological virtues, of course, is not his intention. An examination of *The Spiritual Canticle* and *The Living Flame of Love* makes clear nonetheless that hope, for St. John of the Cross, is not just a tool for purification but an expectant yearning for God that is cleansed and strengthened by the emptying of the memory.[3] Hope, then, plays a critical role both in the heart of the active work of purification and as a person draws near to the living God in deep communion.

Since John of the Cross does not really provide a broad introduction to the virtue of hope before addressing its role in purifying the memory, it may be helpful to contemporary readers for us to provide such an introduction. Drawing on traditional theological reflections on hope in addition to our own experience might help us to see more clearly the unique insights that St. John of the Cross provides for our understanding of the Christian life more broadly.

Hope Looks to the Future

Hope has a fundamental orientation to the future, to what is not yet possessed but what we can expect to possess by God's promise and help. Hope is the expectation that God will

3. Federico Ruiz Salvador, *Místico y maestro: San Juan de la Cruz* (Madrid: Editorial de Espiritualidad, 2006), 269. I find Ruiz's analysis of John's understanding of hope to be particularly helpful, both in his work just cited and also in his earlier book, *Introducción a San Juan de la Cruz: El hombre, los escritos, el sistema* (Madrid: Biblioteca de Autores Cristianos, 1968), 466–71. In English, see Ross Collings, O.C.D., *John of the Cross*, Way of the Mystics 10 (Collegeville, Minn.: Liturgical/Michael Glazier, 1990), 122–33.

accomplish what God has promised, most especially divine union, and the trust that divine help will not be lacking on the journey. Such hope is grounded in faith—faith in God's self-revelation especially in Jesus Christ and faith in the divine invitation made to sinners to share in the divine life. Hope is built on the belief and the trust that God actively desires to make attainable for us what is infinitely beyond our unaided capacities. Grounded in such faith, hope is linked with the love that has been awakened by the Good News that we have been first loved by God. Love awakens love, and because of God's offer and promise in Jesus, we hope to attain the object of our love. Without such hope, we could neither begin the spiritual journey nor be sustained in it.

With a focus always on the future, hope raises our gaze beyond the present, beyond sorrow in what we lack, pain in what we suffer, or passing joy in the things that we possess. True Christian hope orients us to an infinite horizon, to God as God truly is—always more and beyond our understanding or imagining. The theological virtue of hope, therefore, is not an attitude of mere optimism about life nor a general confidence that either we or "fate" will eventually overcome. Christian hope surpasses all such natural hope.

Christian faith reveals that in this life our temptation is often to hope for far too little. Our hoping is narrow and superficial. We hope for a better day. We hope to get beyond the present difficulty. We hope for heaven, conceived as a place just like our earthly existence, only somehow happier and free of difficulty. John of the Cross insists that true Christian hope is directed to a future that is impossible for us even to imagine, much less to accomplish on our own—participation in the divine life itself. And it is such hope that relativizes the present reality, whatever it is, good or ill.

The Problem of Hope in Contemporary Culture

Like the other two theological virtues, hope is both a divine gift and a task to be taken up. Our contemporary culture can present obstacles both to receiving this gift and to working to let it take root in our lives. Certainly, anything that undermines faith also undermines the hope that is grounded in it. Thus, to the degree that living in our culture works against faith, it also makes it more difficult to live in hope.

Today we live in a world of the instantaneous. We expect instant gratification. If our web browser takes more than a second to open, we are irritated by this terrible delay. We have remote controls to move speedily through the hundreds of available channels on satellite television. We grow impatient at a ninety-second wait at a traffic light. We are irritated when people in front of us in the checkout line take the time to write out a check or fumble for their wallets. But Christian hope is not about instant gratification. It involves a patient and trusting—and active—waiting for the unimaginable future that the utterly transcendent God will bring about. How can we truly develop the virtue of hope in a world that expects the instantaneous?

Because hope, as St. John of the Cross emphasizes so frequently, looks to what we do not yet possess, it is hard to live in hope in a world in which we seem to possess so much. At least in many affluent countries, whether we are technically rich or not, we possess more than we need. If we feel that we lack something, we drive to the mall and buy it or get on the Internet and order it. In that sense, we can be too bloated—and thus too blinded—by what we possess to focus much attention on what we lack. We lose sight of the ultimate inadequacy of anything that we can buy, hold, or use up, precisely because once we have bought, held, or used it up, we can go on to the next thing and do the same. How can we hope in a world in which all of our needs and wants seem so easily met? The future direction of hope, with its expectation of possessing the transcendent God, reveals clearly the absolute paltriness of worldly possessions. But sometimes we are so dazzled by the superficial glitz of what we possess or by whatever stands within our grasp that we lose sight of the infinite treasure that could be ours if we would just raise our gaze.

In a similar way, we live in a world in which we can come to believe that any problem can eventually be overcome and any dream attained. We have our own abilities. We have the seemingly daily advances in what technology can do. Eventually, we're led to believe, there will be a pill to cure whatever ails us (and even prevent what *might* eventually ail us). It's easy, then, to hope in ourselves, to hope in progress, to hope in what science will arrive at next. This is a kind of hubris, a kind of pride that is antithetical to hope. It will, of course, eventually confront the reality of a suffering that cannot be overcome, a disease that cannot be cured, the death that cannot be held at bay. But day to day, in our normal lives, such pride without true Christian hope is a trap we can fall into all too easily.

The Contraries of Hope: Discouragement and Despair

The opposite of hope is, of course, discouragement and despair. With these, there is no expectation that things will get better. It is not possible to overcome the present situation. There is no better future to which one can dare to look. In the face of obstacles and failure, there is no hope, just perhaps the willpower to carry on, wait it out, and "hope" that "things will work out." In the spiritual life, it is easy for sincere Christians to fall into a spirit of discouragement as we face sins that cannot be easily overcome, regardless of how sincere our efforts or how heartfelt our prayer.

Such discouragement and despair is grounded precisely in the false trust that we have placed in ourselves, in other mortals, or in our merely human abilities. If our hope is not in what God can do and in what God has promised, if our horizon is not broader than our hopes for this passing life, discouragement is the inevitable end of our efforts. If we have no Christian hope, if our hoping is narrow, if our horizons are limited, we will inevitably walk in discouragement or be tempted to despair.

Having served for several years as a pastor and having accompanied many through the loss of loved ones, I can say, what a difference there is between the grief of those who have Christian faith and hope . . . and those who do not! Grief at the death of those we love is profoundly human. For the Christian, however, grief is tempered at a deeper level by hope in what Jesus has promised. It is no wonder that the church's funeral rites include so many hope-filled texts. The righteous Job proclaims in the midst of his dire suffering, "For I know that my Redeemer lives, and that at the last he will stand upon the earth; and after my skin has been thus destroyed, then in my flesh I shall see God" (Job 19:25-26). In the middle of the woeful lamentations that give the Old Testament book its title, its author begins, "The thought of my affliction and my homelessness is wormwood and gall!" but one verse later he continues, "But this I call to mind, and therefore I hope: The steadfast love of the Lord never ceases, his mercies never come to an end; they are new every morning; great is your faithfulness" (Lam 3:19, 21–23).

In his 2007 encyclical on hope, *Spe Salvi* (In Hope We Were Saved), Pope Benedict XVI speaks of suffering as the testing ground and the school of hope (nos. 35–40). Our response to

the inevitable and sometimes unavoidable experience of suffering shows how deeply rooted our hope really is—or perhaps is
not. Such suffering invites us to hold more firmly to God's gift of
hope. Suffering teaches us—because often it forces us—to hope
in what God can accomplish that we cannot. More, it challenges
us to look beyond every suffering as well as every good thing that
this life has to offer. God is infinitely more, and the sharing in
the divine life that God offers is beyond our ability even to grasp.

Even in the spiritual life, the discouragement of the sincere
Christian reveals a failure of hope. We become discouraged
because we have failed, because we have not lived up to our
expectations, because we have not yet arrived at the sinlessness
that is our goal. But Christian hope is precisely hope in God's
mercy, hope in what God can accomplish, and hope in the gift
of salvation that God will ultimately give even to the greatest of
saints. Spiritual discouragement is the inevitable result of the
Christian who has placed his or her hope in self. Hope calls us to
place all things in God's hands, pick oneself up, and get back on
course to the future that God makes possible through the divine
mercy and help. Christian hope, then, must always walk hand in
hand with humility.

With true Christian hope comes peace. As St. Paul says, "We
know that all things work together for good for those who love
God" (Rom 8:28)—which is to say that God is at work "behind
the scenes," as it were, to bring the good and the bad together
into the unimaginable possibilities that the divine will seeks to
accomplish. In discussing how hope purifies the memory, John
of the Cross notes that our anxieties and worries are formed
from the woeful imaginings drawn together from images in
our memories. Hope, he tells us, brings peace precisely by calm-
ing our anxieties: "Thus if the whole world were to crumble
and come to an end and all things were to go wrong, it would

be useless to get disturbed, for this would do more harm than good" (A.3.6.3).[4] Hope would bring tranquility and calm even in the midst of it all.

The Enemy of Hope: Presumption

The authentic Christian life is grounded in faith in the God who loves us and in the future that God holds in store for those who respond with love. The Christian journey, then, is a walking in hope that God will enable us to love beyond our limited and creaturely capacity.

Presumption is the enemy of hope. It is the easy assumption that God will simply give us salvation with no real effort on our part to respond to the incredible divine gift. But it is not authentic Christian hope to live our daily lives just as we choose and then to expect that God will simply give us either union with the divine in this life or complete union with the Trinity in the life to come. Yes, salvation is ultimately a gift even for the greatest saint, and God does will the salvation of us all. All of the theological virtues by which we can direct our lives to God are gifts. But we must respond to the divine self-offer, not once but throughout our lives. We must cooperate with God's work of conforming us to the divine will so that we mere humans—sinful humans—can truly become friends of God, suited to receive the divine life in our humanity.

When I was a pastor, I often wondered at the fact that every single person at a crowded Sunday Mass could receive

---

4. Marc Foley notes that John offers the same comment in a number of places in his writing, suggesting the apparent importance of this idea for maintaining tranquility of soul and hope even through life's difficulties. Marc Foley, O.C.D., *The Ascent of Mount Carmel: Reflections* (Washington, D.C.: ICS Publications, 2013), 153.

Communion. Of course, participation in the sacrament is a great good to be encouraged for everyone, and I am not in a position to judge the worthiness of anyone else to share in the Eucharist. At the same time, I wondered sometimes if there isn't a spirit of presumption at work in our eucharistic assemblies. I don't mean to encourage a sense of scrupulosity about sin or to suggest that we must go to confession before every reception of Communion. My point is that it is one thing to trust in God's merciful love toward sinners as we receive the Lord's body and blood (which we must all do). It is quite another thing to presume on that mercy and love by giving no thought to whether my life outside of the Eucharist is compatible with communion with Christ and his people. This is no different from distinguishing between trusting in my spouse's love for me despite my failings and, on the other hand, presuming on that love by assuming that I can do whatever I want without consequence to our relationship.

I wondered likewise at the many funeral liturgies in which neither the deceased nor the mourners had darkened the door of a church in years. Again, even the most holy among us cannot claim a right to heaven. Ultimately, we must all trust in God's mercy. And still it seemed a bit presumptuous to think that these funeral prayers that speak of hope that the deceased even now shares in eternal life would necessarily apply to someone who seemingly thought so little of God in this life. Of course, happily for a pastor and for anyone who might fall under his merely human judgment, there is always the possibility of a conversion at the last moment and the assurance that God the merciful judge will sort it all out on the other side of death. And still, might these situations not be another example of the possibility of presumption—that is, the opposite of true Christian hope?

Of course, there is hardly a greater danger of presumption than among us "professional" religious folks—we who have devoted our lives to God and have "given up so much for God." Perhaps it is all too easy to presume that the externals of our religious lives—what might be sometimes just going through the motions or done halfheartedly—will somehow guarantee our eternal participation in the divine life. Like the people mentioned in the previous paragraphs who might be too casual about their relationship with God and take God's mercy for granted, we religious professionals can face the same temptation.

Hope is not presumption. As St. John of the Cross teaches us, true Christian hope deepens our longing for God and strengthens our resolve even as we humbly trust in what God's love must accomplish in us.

The Memory Must Be Emptied

> In the measure that the memory becomes dispossessed of things, in that measure it will have hope, and the more hope it has the greater will be its union with God; for in relation to God, the more a soul hopes the more it attains. (A.3.7.2)

Our reflection on the broader discussion of Christian hope provides a context in which to place the thought of St. John of the Cross on hope. But, at the same time, John's thought takes us deeper into what hope can do—and, in fact, what hope *must* do if we wish truly to enter into union with God in this life.

In *The Ascent of Mount Carmel*, John focuses on the purification of the memory through the theological virtue of hope, which must accompany the purification of the intellect by faith and of the will by love. His identification of the purifying role of hope, especially in its relation to memory, is both unique and deeply insightful. It is important, then, to look more closely at how he understands the memory and at how the memory can be an obstacle in the spiritual life and ultimately a hindrance to divine union. Only then will we be able to truly appreciate the relationship that he sees between the two.

The Function of the Memory

As we saw in our introduction to the theological virtues, Thomas Aquinas, whose thought John studied at the University of Salamanca, held that there are two faculties: intellect and will. John, however, reflecting the distinctively Augustinian emphasis of the Carmelite theology of his time, speaks of three faculties (or powers or capacities) of the human soul: intellect, will, and memory. (For Aquinas, memory is an aspect of the intellect.) Again, as we have seen, John evidently felt free to draw from many sources. It is not clear if his acceptance of the threefold division is a theological and philosophical conviction that he firmly held, or simply a kind of construct that allows him to focus more attention on the theological virtue of hope than the Thomistic twofold division might have permitted.[5]

It is perhaps missed easily enough, but in speaking of the purification or emptying of the memory, John is not suggesting that we should simply try to forget everything we know or "erase our memory banks." This is neither desirable nor possible. The danger with memory is not in *having* memories, retained images, or remembering tasks we need to do. The problem is *attachment* to such things in the memory or being distracted by them: "Thus people are not required to stop recalling and thinking about what they must do and know, for, if they are not attached to the possession of these thoughts, they will not be harmed" (A.3.15.1).

---

5. Ruiz, *Introducción a San Juan de la Cruz*, 467.

What, then, does purification of memory mean if it does not simply mean forgetting everything? To answer this question, it is important to see that for John the memory is a power or capacity. It is not merely a passive storehouse of memories.[6] It is not the storehouse that has to be emptied but rather the capacity and tendency to bring memories and images to consciousness that must be purified or emptied.

Further, we must understand that for John, memory and imagination work together closely.[7] The function of the faculty of memory is not just in calling to mind images or concepts from the past and thus potentially being distracted or becoming attached to them; it is also the function of memory to draw from images and experiences of the past to imagine new possibilities. The work of the imagination depends on memory in order to think of alternative possibilities, envision the future, and to conceive of realities that have not yet been personally experienced. For example, I have never seen a unicorn, but even without artistic renderings I could imagine one from my stored images of horses and horns. In a similar way, I can imagine all sorts of future possibilities to distract me or to which I can become attached, drawn from images and experiences of the past. Again, it is not the images or memories themselves that are the problem but drawing them into consciousness and dwelling on them—precisely at the time that God is calling the person into imageless contemplation.

---

6. Kieran Kavanaugh, O.C.D., *John of the Cross: Doctor of Light and Love*, Spiritual Legacy Series (New York: Crossroad, 1999), 155. See also Collings, *John of the Cross*, 125.

7. The relationship of memory and imagination is more complex and even obscure in John's thought, though this complexity need not concern us for our purposes here. Just a few words of explanation: For him, there are "interior" senses that exist between our "exterior senses" (sight, smell, touch, etc.) and our faculties or powers (intellect, memory, and will). Among these interior senses are sense memory (distinct from the faculty of memory), imagination, and phantasy. These last two are related in their operation, so John often treats them as one. See *The Collected Works*, 185n1, and specific references to these senses in the Glossary of Terms, 770, 772, 773. See also Foley, *Ascent of Mount Carmel*, 3–6.

We have just seen, in a broad way, the meaning of both hope and memory. Since John's reflection on memory is at times dense, it might be useful to look at some of the problems with memory that we can recognize in our own experience. What are some of the problems with a disorderly or controlling memory? Having reflected on our own experience of memory, we will have a better sense of why John of the Cross teaches that memory must be purified by hope.

The Many Problematic Faces of Memory

We probably have never given much thought to any ways that our memories might weigh us down or hold us back, as St. John of the Cross is suggesting. At the same time, we get a sense of this reality immediately when we hear of people who are "carrying baggage from their past," "living in the past," "dwelling on the past," or who "can't let go of the past." Perhaps there are some people who tend to dwell too much on "the way things were" or the "good ol' days" and thereby close themselves to blessings in the present or new possibilities in the future. Similarly, there are people—and this probably describes many of us, at least sometimes—who tend to hold on to past hurts, who remember every apparent offense or slight, or who can't let go of mistakes that they themselves made. In instances such as these, we can readily see how memory can be problematic, holding us back or paralyzing us. Hope, as John of the Cross suggests, looks to the future and can therefore redirect our orientation beyond the past and beyond the present. We can already see, at this level, the liberating possibilities of hope.

Often the experience of holding on to past hurts is like replaying an old video of moments in which we were embarrassed or disrespected. Our sense of hurt at the time may have been quite real and intense, but it is in the past. Our memory, though, replays these images and experiences with their accompanying feelings of anger, frustration, or belittlement, and it does so for no good, constructive purpose. We are living in the present, but our present living and relating is somehow stuck in the past. Perhaps there is no way realistically to eradicate these memories, but what we can do is to choose not to replay the images. The problem is not that we have such hurtful memories in our "memory banks," needing to be erased. The problem is that we recall them, and they distract us or grab hold of us so we cannot move forward. In short, we find ourselves in need of the healing power of forgiveness. This might be a matter not of forgetting but of refusing to hit the Play button on our memories. More deeply, we can choose to replay the memories but with Jesus in prayer, asking to be free of them and hoping in the Spirit's power to accomplish the liberation and healing in us that we seem unable to do on our own.

The old manuals of moral theology provide another hint to the sometimes problematic experience of memory. These manuals were used as textbooks in seminaries before the Second Vatican Council, and they often included the careful identification of multiple classes and degrees of sin. One particular sin that involves the memory is called "sinful joy." This involves the intentional recollection of an evil committed in the past, which one is resolved never to commit again, but the person takes pleasure in recalling the sin. Certainly, the manuals can be criticized for a spirit of legalism and even scrupulosity, but, at the same time, "sinful joy" reveals another way that memory can sabotage us.

Of course, one doesn't carry out any external action in "sinful joy." But there is choice—the choice of whether to recall and to hold on to something that was evil in the past. The person doesn't repeat that external action of the past in the present, but by choosing to ponder it again, the memory takes on a new life within the one who intentionally holds on to it. It exists again in the one who chooses to remember, though this time without external manifestation. The memory, then, makes evil come alive again. Like someone with a weakened immune system, due to these dangerous memories the person is now more liable to indulge in these thoughts and might even be in danger of committing similar actions in the present or in the future.

Precisely in this vein, St. John of the Cross notes that memories engender appetites and attachment (A.3.3.3–4). He quotes a saying: "What the eye doesn't see, the heart doesn't want" (A.3.5.1). Memories can awaken disordered and unruly appetites, stimulating emotions of desire, joy, or sorrow, and threatening the tranquility and inner order that is the necessary condition for deep prayer and the ordered life (A.3.5.2–3). The imagination can draw on memory to conjure up images and possibilities that lead to anxiety and worry, when it would be best simply to trust and to hope in peace (A.3.6.3).

Memory is also related to the reality that every person of prayer knows all too well: distractions. The advice that St. John of the Cross and St. Teresa of Avila offer about distractions in prayer is to pay them no mind. Let them go. The important thing is not to grab hold of them—or let them grab hold of us—as they float by in our consciousness where they can do us no harm. John's analysis of the memory makes clear that the images and thoughts that constitute our distractions flow from the memory or from imagination's use of memory. Memories in themselves are not the problem, just as having distractions in prayer is not the problem. The problem is with allowing ourselves to be distracted by them or becoming attached to them. It is in the context of John's discussion of the active night of spirit that he speaks of memory. We see more clearly that an active memory produces images, including even holy images and recollections of spiritual encounters. But in fact even these are distractions to the person being invited into imageless contemplation.

Memory and Hope

Our broader reflections of hope and memory allow us, at last, to look at how St. John of the Cross understands the relationship between the two. For him, memory is about possession, while hope is about what is not yet possessed. Hope is openness to a future that is always beyond our grasp. Memory is full of images and experiences that we possess, ready to be retrieved, mulled over, and formed into new images and thoughts. For that reason, memory clearly has an important function in normal daily living. But the point comes in one's deepening relationship with God when the memory and its focus on possessing get in the way. In discussing the theological virtue of faith, we have already seen that the utter transcendence of God means that God is beyond any possible knowledge or concept that we might have. We must walk in dark faith, increasingly stripped of our limited notions and concepts about a limitless God. So too with memory and hope. The memory must be emptied; its tendency to recall images and to focus our attention on them must be put to sleep, because these memories, even of the most sublime spiritual experiences and encounters in our past, are always infinitely less than God. Just as the intellect must walk in the darkness of faith, so too the memory must walk in the emptiness of hope.

Hope always looks to what is not possessed. The infinite and transcendent God who is drawing us into divine union is always beyond our grasp. If we content ourselves with dwelling on spiritual images, memories, and imaginings—much less allowing ourselves to become bogged down by more mundane, hurtful, or even sinful memories—then we shall never be a vessel truly empty to receive the gift of the abiding presence of the living God. God alone is a "possession" worth having or striving for. We can be possessed by God only in the emptiness in which we are truly free to surrender completely to the divine embrace.

For St. John of the Cross, the problem of memory goes to the root of our identity—who or what we suppose ourselves to be.[8] We human beings are historical beings. Not only do we live in history—in time that passes through a series of events, some intentional, some random—but we also *are* a history. We live *in* history, and we *are* a history of what we have done and what has been done to us, our sins and our acts of love, our triumphs and our failures. In Catholic moral theology, we say that we constitute ourselves—we make ourselves to be certain kinds of people—by the choices we make, the acts that we choose, and the omissions of things that we might have done. Certainly, this is clearest in the way that we "construct" ourselves (necessarily aided, of course, by God's grace in every good act) through the series of positive decisions by which we grow in the habitual dispositions, the abiding tendencies, that we call virtues. It is also tragically true that we make ourselves through the bad actions by which we form in ourselves vices that separate us from God and from one another.

Memory too plays an important role in this construction of a self and particularly in the construction of our self-identity. We can say that we possess our memories. But more accurately,

8. My reflection on memory and self-possession has benefited greatly from Collings, *John of the Cross*, 127–28, and the two works by Ruiz: *Místico y maestro*, 272–73, and *Introducción a San Juan de la Cruz*, 469. A brief introduction to the Augustinian foundation of John's discussion of memory and its relationship to self-identity is offered by Dominic Doyle, "Changing Hopes: The Theological Virtue of Hope in Thomas Aquinas, John of the Cross, and Karl Rahner," *Irish Theological Quarterly* 77 (February 2012): 24–29.

we can say that our identities are formed by these memories. We know who we are through our memories of where, how, and who we have been. We understand ourselves in relation to the images, experiences, and concepts that we can conjure up at any moment. We know ourselves through the memories of people we have encountered in life—the ones who have loved us and whom we have loved; the ones who have influenced us for good or ill. Memory, as John of the Cross says, is about possession. What memory most fundamentally enables us to possess is ourselves. Memory is the foundation of our daily self-possession.

Normally we also look to our future from the foothold of our memories. We imagine how our future might be and how we could be in the future by drawing from our experiences of the past. Whether we are optimistic about the future and can imagine a better self yet to come or pessimistic and see ourselves burdened by woe and failure, we are depending importantly on memory and imagination in projecting any future.

Memory plays a similar role in our so-called spiritual lives. Our sense of our relationship with God, who we understand ourselves to be before God, where we stand at any moment in the eyes of God, our "spiritual identity," our identity as Christians—all of these are formed by memory. The memory is also at work as we envision the spiritual path before us. We imagine and set out to grow closer to God according to what we have read and been taught, what spiritual friends and mentors have told or shown us, how the saints have lived, and what we have experienced of God in the past.

But the infinite and transcendent God is always calling us to more. God is calling us to become more. At every moment God is calling us to our true identity, united with Christ in God's own life, which ultimately we cannot even understand, conceive, or imagine.

It is for this reason that memory gets in the way. What has formed us to this moment becomes a hindrance, an obstacle. We cannot embrace the unimaginable future that God has in store for us and the true identity that God wants to give us if we hold on to what our memories have made us or what we imagine we might become. If memory once fulfilled the necessary task of forming an identity and if it serves as the basis from which we can imagine a future, the time comes when it must be put to sleep because it is a roadblock to what God truly wants for us. If our so-called spiritual lives and our spiritual ideals and goals were once formed by what we learned, were taught, and saw modeled for us, we must now put it all aside. Because God is more. God calls us to more. God calls us to be more through union with and within the divine life itself.

The theological virtue of hope is God's gift to us to look ahead to a future and to an identity beyond our conceiving. We must embrace this gift, and with God's constant help we must allow it to empty the memory, turn off the constant flow of memory, so that memory no longer holds us back, no longer directs us to what is less than God. Hope looks to what is not yet possessed. It looks forward to what we are meant to become. We must allow hope to dismantle our constricted sense of self built on memory. We must embrace its power to explode our narrow imaginings of a future constructed from images from the past. Christian hope is directed to an infinite future and to our participation in the life of an utterly transcendent God. Our intellects cannot grasp such a future. Our imaginations cannot conceive it. We must instead surrender to it. We must hope, that is, embrace the divine gift of hope and wield it as a weapon against what enslaves us to the past, distracts us in the present, or limits us to a path that leads merely to a constricted future of our own human conceiving.

Hope Beyond the Active Night

Where have you hidden,
Beloved, and left me moaning?

Canticle, stanza 1

St. John of the Cross's reflection on the purifying role of hope in the active night of spirit does not exhaust his sense of hope's purpose in the Christian journey. Hope does not merely purify. Hope is the constant and vibrant force that compels the human person toward a share in the divine life that God has definitively offered and made accessible in Jesus Christ. Faith reveals the gift and promise of participation in the life of God. Hope, born of faith's vision, drives the person always forward to attain what is the only true and ultimate fulfillment of any and every human life. In faith, divine love has been revealed. Love awakens love, and hope impels the person forward to the attainment of love's desiring. Hope looks to the fullness of life in God and will settle for nothing less. Hope dares to pursue what is simply impossible for mere human beings, that is, to give ourselves completely and without reserve to God and to respond to the divine love with an equal love. But such an impossibility can only be possible if the person has become empty of self so that by the divine indwelling God can love God in us.[9]

Even in the heights of union attainable in this life, hope looks to a still greater participation in the triune life, in the life of glory. Hope's characteristic orientation and longing for the future continually pushes and expands love in its longing for more. "Moaning is connected with hope" (C.1.14), comments John of the Cross in reflecting on love for God that can find no satisfaction in this life. The soul loves so intensely—and so hopes for full union with God in glory—that it moans with love;

---

9. Ruiz, *Introducción a San Juan de la Cruz*, 470–71.

it moans in hope. One is sublimely "wounded" with a love that cannot find a healing completion until the fullness for which it hopes is attained beyond the veil that separates this life from the next (C.1.17). Commenting on the first stanza of *The Living Flame of Love*, John describes the profound sigh that rises from the soul in deepest union as it longs for a yet-to-be-realized final consummation. Even when the soul has arrived at the deepest union that is possible in this life, "it still lives in hope" (F.1.27).

If, in the course of the Christian journey, the purifying work of hope is at times "wearying," it nonetheless looks ahead with a deep yearning, at every stage of the Christian journey, to what mere mortals cannot imagine or deserve:

> By this bright hope
> which came to them from above,
> their wearying labors
> were lightened;
> but the drawn-out waiting
> and their growing desire
> to rejoice with their Bridegroom
> wore on them continually.
> So, with prayers
> and sighs and suffering,
> with tears and moanings
> they asked night and day
> that now he would determine
> to grant them his company.
>
> *Romances* 5

For Questions for Reflection / Discussion see pages 156–157

6 Love

You shall love the Lord, your God, with all your heart, and with all your soul, and with all your strength [Dt 6:5]. This passage contains all that spiritual persons must do and all I must teach them here if they are to reach God by union of the will through charity. In it human beings receive the command to employ all the faculties, appetites, operations, and emotions of their soul in God so that they will use all this ability and strength for nothing else, in accord with David's words: *Fortitudinem meam ad te custodiam* (I will keep my strength for you) [Ps 59:10]. (A.3.16.1)

With these words St. John of the Cross summarizes what he will say about the purifying work of the theological virtue of love in the latter half of book 3 of *The Ascent of Mount Carmel* (A.3.16–45). The gift of love, by which God empowers us to love in response, moves us, through the power of the purified will, to focus all of our desires and energy on our self-giving to God in love. Just as John's discussion of hope focused more on the memory being in need of emptying, he looks here most especially at the disordered affections that must be brought into order by the purified will. While in *The Spiritual Canticle* and *The Living Flame of Love*, as in his poetry, John sings the beauty of the love that unites us to God, here in *The Ascent*, his focus is on love's power to purify and order our affections.

As we did in looking at John's discussion of faith and hope, it will be useful to focus on a broader context for understanding what John of the Cross has to say about desire, the will, virtues, and love.

Desire and Choice

A superficial reading of *The Ascent of Mount Carmel* suggests that John of the Cross has an inherently negative view of human desire, but a closer look reveals that this is not the case at all.[1] To desire is fundamentally human. To be human is to desire. In fact, the Catholic moral tradition—as taught by St. Thomas Aquinas and familiar to John of the Cross—makes clear that all the good things that God has created and that we naturally desire are in some way a reflection of the divine reality. Every created thing bears some trace of God, even if only in the smallest way. No wonder that we can be overcome with a sense of the divine grandeur as we look out on natural beauty, whether it is the immensity of the ocean or a night sky illuminated by the moon and countless stars. John expresses this truth poetically in the fifth stanza of his poem *The Spiritual Canticle*. Here the soul tells of how the Beloved has left his image implanted in nature:

---

1. John of the Cross uses various terms for what I am broadly calling desire—such as (in English) appetite, affection, emotion, passion. There are nuances of difference in the use of each term—for John and especially in the broader Scholastic thought of his time—but he does not define the terms, and it really would not serve his purpose. Fundamentally, whatever the term, his focus is on the fact that by nature we are beings who desire, and this desiring can become disordered and must be made right by an active and all-embracing love in the will. See Federico Ruiz Salvador, *Introducción a San Juan de la Cruz: El hombre, los escritos, el sistema* (Madrid: Biblioteca de Autores Cristianos, 1968), 581–82.

Pouring out a thousand graces,
he passed these groves in haste;
and having looked at them,
with his image alone,
clothed them in beauty. (C.5)

His Carmelite brothers reported that John often could be found gazing out a window or sitting in the midst of nature, rapt in wonder.

Created goods reflect God, and God has created us so that we are naturally drawn to them. We naturally desire them. We desire food, because food is fundamentally good for us; and food and the act of eating point to God as the source of our sustenance. In faith we see that ordinary food and the ordinary act of eating become symbols of the superabundance of heaven understood through an analogy of eating at a lavish banquet. The most basic goods that God has created are a reflection of the divine; they are good for us. In choosing the good, we are implicitly choosing God in some small way and choosing what is really for our good. On the other hand, to choose against such a good is also to harm ourselves and to act against what God commands, precisely because the divine will is always for our good.

Desire, then, is born of our need. We are limited and incomplete. Satisfied for a time, our need arises again. We discover that no sooner is one need met when we have another. We need food and drink and shelter. We also need friendship and a sense of meaning. At the heart of mortal and limited humanity there is a most basic incompleteness and desiring. Above all, we need God. In fact, at the foundation of all of our desiring is our desire for God. We might catch a glimpse of God in these created goods, but it is God alone who can satisfy our desiring.

In St. Thomas Aquinas's framework, desire moves us to the good; our intellect helps us to discern if the good to which we are drawn is truly a good for us in this situation, and the will chooses to act according to what the intellect has discerned. Sadly, because of the reality of sin, this divinely ordered plan can break down at any number of points. Our desires can be disordered and thus move us toward things that are not good and away from what is authentically good; sin can so cloud our intellect that we cannot discern what is truly good; and our will can be too weak to choose the truly good even if our intellect is able to recognize it. The intellect is meant to be the guide for our right desiring, but sometimes the intellect is blinded by sin or our will is too weak to choose the good. Our lives are then misguided by our disordered desires (A.1.8.3). Even the famously wise King Solomon was led astray into foolishness and sin because "his affection for women and his neglect to deny the appetites and delights of his heart" got the best of him (A.1.8.6).

In teaching about the purifying work of the theological virtue of love, John focuses particularly on the reality of our disordered desire and how love for God active in the will must bring order and unity to our desiring and choosing. Our desire needs to be single-hearted and focused: we must desire God above all and in all and desire all things in God, rather than having a multitude of desires, in which one among the many is a desire for God. In other words, God is not one object among many, just bigger or more important. God is the authentic goal of all of our desiring and the satisfaction of every desire. We must desire God above all and in all, and we must choose God above all in love. John's explicit focus in this part of *The Ascent* is on our desire, because it is the will that should direct the desires by rightly guiding our choices and actions, as illuminated by a clear-sighted intellect. It is only the divine gift of the theological virtue of love that can ultimately cleanse and empower the will so that it can properly order all of our desiring to God.

When our desires are purified, then all of their energy is focused together in a wholehearted love for God: "The strength of the soul comprises the faculties, passions, and appetites. All this strength is ruled by the will. When the will directs these faculties, passions, and appetites toward God, turning away from all that is not God, the soul preserves its strength for God, and comes to love him with all its might" (A.3.16.2). It is as if our desire were a river meant to flow into union with God; yet our desires are disordered, so that much of the water is being diverted from its principal channel into little streams that flow here and there. The great channel that should propel us toward union with God is then often at best a trickle. Love must empower the will to direct the water once again into a torrent that can propel us toward God, who alone can satisfy all of our needs and desires.

Disordered Desire

The enemy along the path to divine union is not desire in itself but *disordered* desire. The problem is not the good things outside of ourselves but rather the disorder within us. Following the Scholastic framework of his time, John describes the disordered passions in this way: "A person then very easily rejoices in what deserves no rejoicing, hopes for what brings no profit, sorrows over what should perhaps cause rejoicing, and fears where there is no reason for fear" (A.3.16.4). It does not require a deep understanding of the Scholastic identification of the four passions of joy, hope, sorrow, and fear to appreciate this picture of disordered affection. When our desires are rightly ordered, we rejoice in what is authentically good for us, not in what is a

merely passing pleasure that it not truly good or that might ultimately harm us. We should hope to attain those things that will
authentically fulfill us, and we should regret the lack of what is
truly good rather than grieving the absence of what is merely
superficial or even evil. We should fear what could truly harm
us rather than fear being deprived of what is unnecessary or ultimately harmful.

When these passions are not under the direction of the will,
we lack the authentic human integrity that leads to real fulfillment. In sum, John offers a fundamental principle: "The will
should rejoice only in what is for the honor and glory of God,
and the greatest honor we can give him is to serve him according
to evangelical perfection; anything unincluded in such service is
without value to human beings" (A.3.17.2). Or, as he says later
in the text, "There is nothing worthy of a person's joy save the
service of God and the procurement of his honor and glory in
all things" (A.3.20.3). Union with God is our fulfillment, and all
value is measured against this most fundamental truth.

A good deal of John's discussion of the role of love in purifying the will is focused on disordered desire, or passions. In fact,
although he states that he will address all four of the passions
(joy, hope, sorrow, and fear), he never gets beyond a discussion
of joy! *The Ascent* ends rather abruptly, obviously unfinished.
Still, in the course of examining the many levels and kinds of
material and spiritual goods in which we can rejoice, John offers
some important insight into the nature and consequences of disordered desire. Clearly, desire focused on things less than God
distracts us from our path to divine union. Speaking specifically
about disordered desire for material goods, but applicable more
broadly to our desires for less tangible goods, John cautions
that disordered joy leads to progressive withdrawing from God
and therefore a deterioration of the spiritual life and of focus

(A.3.19.1). The list of negative effects of disordered joy goes on: the darkening of the mind and judgment about what is truly valuable, cooling of spiritual fervor, dissipation of our commitment, a lukewarm spirit, mere formality in spiritual practice, and ultimately abandoning God for worship of "other gods."

Doesn't this analysis, even though couched in the Scholastic terminology of his time, ring true to our experience? It is simply a sad fact that—whether in sixteenth-century Spain or in twenty-first-century America—focusing our energy on what is less than God diminishes or dissipates our commitment and zeal for God and for the things of God. John of the Cross offers a great deal of moral and spiritual insight as he analyzes the harms of seeking joy in anything less than God as well as the benefits of raising our gaze to God who is the source of goodness and beauty.

In looking at the nature of virtue in a previous chapter, we saw how acquired moral virtues grow over time through one choice after another. The vices too grow in this way, and what John is describing can be seen as the moral and spiritual deterioration that comes from disordered desires and their effects. Disordered desire leads us to one bad choice and action after another; our will is thereby weakened in its ability to choose the good. Our virtues are undermined, our vices grow, and sin deepens its grasp. Thus, what began as a simple disordered desire can become slavery to sin. As he says, "Through the practice of one virtue all the virtues grow, and similarly, through an increase of one vice, all the vices and their effects grow" (A.1.12.5).

It is no coincidence that one of the classic definitions of sin, from St. Augustine through St. Thomas, is "a turning away from God and a turning toward creatures" (*aversio a Deo et conversio ad creaturam*). Sin means that we have turned away from a foundational orientation of our life to God and chosen instead to direct ourselves to something that can neither fulfill us nor bring us true and lasting joy. This misdirection is rooted precisely in the disordered desire that pulls us away from the good that leads to God.

Virtue and Ordered Desire

The will must bring the delinquent desires back into order. This is the work of the theological virtue of love, which directs our will and thus our desires to God, who is the proper goal of our desiring. This process, as we saw when we looked at the difficult path of the active night of the senses, is challenging and even painful, but it leads to the freedom to live as we were meant to do.

At a simple human level, ordered desire brings an inner calm and harmony. Our desires are no longer pulling us in different directions. We no longer feel like the slaves of our appetites. This is the work of the virtue of temperance, which brings balance and order and thus a tranquil spirit. Like all of the natural moral virtues, it is acquired by our effort aided by the working of grace. At the same time, according to St. Thomas, God infuses us with special virtues to give us yet more empowerment to properly order our desire and to conform our inner life with our most fundamental desire for God—the desire that, in fact, is the root of all of our desiring.

In the monastic tradition, this integration of desire is called purity of heart. It describes the inner life of a person who has attained the balance and thus the tranquility of ordered desiring. This is the necessary precondition to love. We cannot truly love while we are pushed and pulled in different directions, when our appetites move us to selfish fulfillment while love demands selfless giving. When our hearts are made pure so that we can desire what is truly good for ourselves and for others, we are then truly free to love both God and our neighbor (A.3.20.4).[2]

When we have been freed of our disorder and our attachments, we will be able to truly appreciate and enjoy the things of this world as they were meant to be appreciated. In fact, dispossession, detachment, and ordered desire enable us truly to rejoice in the goodness of things as they truly are (A.3.20.2). United with Christ, loving as Christ loves, we will be able to enjoy and even possess things without being possessed by them. In his "Prayer of a Soul Taken with Love," in *The Sayings of Light and Love*, John offers us, from the perspective of the person in union with God, a sense of the authentic relationship of the person to God and to the creation: "Mine are the heavens and mine is the earth. Mine are the nations, and the just are mine, and mine the sinners. The angels are mine, and the Mother of God, and all things are mine; and God himself is mine and for me, because Christ is mine and for me. What do you ask, then, and seek, my soul? Yours is all of this, and all is for you. Do not engage yourself in something less or pay heed to the crumbs that fall from your Father's table." In this almost ecstatic hymn of the goodness of creation and the richness of the soul authentically free to embrace it, St. John shows us the fruit of right ordering of self, God, and all other things or goods.

Although his contemporaries described John of the Cross as a very loving person in his relationships with others—as is evident in his extant letters—John gives scant explicit attention to love of neighbor in his writings. This is simply not his focus. Our disordered desire and its accompanying focus on self is as much an enemy of true love of neighbor as it is the enemy of love

---

2. José Damian Gaitan, *Negación y plenitud en San Juan de la Cruz* (Madrid: Editorial de Espiritualidad, 1995), 283–84.

for God. Thus, the liberation that comes with the ordering of desire frees us truly to love God and our neighbor with a generous and selfless love. To truly and freely love God also empowers us to freely and authentically love other men and women. John tells us that "as the love of neighbor increases so does the love of God, and as the love of God increases so does the love of neighbor, for what proceeds from God has one and the same reason and cause" (A.3.23.1).

Love Purifies the Will

St. Thomas Aquinas defines love, or charity, as friendship with God because it involves a mutual self-communication and self-giving. By this love, we love God as God is in the divine reality and thus above all. At the same time, we love ourselves and our neighbor within this love.[3] Love, then, is essentially relational, self-giving, and open to receive. As is so typical of his approach, John does not offer us a clear definition of love. It is nonetheless evident that for him, love is grounded in God's gracious self-communication and invitation and our commitment to respond with a similar self-giving. Love understood in this way makes demands on us. The effort to love God with a true openness to receive the divine self-offer and to respond is a difficult task in light of our sin and inner disorder. Disordered desire impedes the ability of our will to love as we should, whereas God's gift of the theological virtue of love empowers the will to order our desires so that we can love freely and even passionately.

St. John of the Cross tells us that to desire two things at once is to make them equivalent to one another, even if one deserves more to be desired. To desire God and to desire anything else

---

3. *Summa Theologiae*, II–II, q.23, a.1.

at the same time is to place God on the same level as, or even lower than, a created good. To love something alongside God is to fail to properly esteem God since we would be equating God with a created object (A.1.4). This would be absurd since God is not merely an object alongside others—not simply something greater or more wonderful—but the Creator and ground of all objects.

In giving us the gift of the theological virtue of love, God provides us with the instrument by which to purify and rightly order our desiring. Love, of course, is more than a tool for purification, but this work of cleansing is the focus of the active night of spirit. Put differently, to the degree that we truly love God, we lift our gaze above or through everything that is less than God. The more we love God, the less we can love anything else in itself. To the degree that we truly love God wholly, then, we can be free enough to love rightly our neighbors and the rest of the created order.

Surely this is the meaning of love within the sacrament of marriage. Married people are not asked to love God rather than one another. They are invited instead to truly love God and to love each other precisely in this deep love expressed in marriage. God is neither an object nor even another human being. When we love one person, our love is necessarily lessened or pulled away from another. But the same cannot be said of our love for God. God is the ground of all being and all true loving, and true love for God is the foundation and vantage point from which we can freely and authentically love everyone and everything else. Loving God does not constrict or limit our ability to love; rather, when it is authentic, love of God enlarges and expands our love of other people and of all creation.

The theological virtue of love, like faith and hope, is a gift, a gift that must be embraced. What is given in grace is not a onetime feeling or decision but a habit, an abiding disposition to love God. But because of sin and disordered desire, acting from this habit, embracing it more deeply, and living it more consistently is sometimes very hard work. In this sense, we can speak of a "dry" love that functions like dark faith.[4] We may not always *feel* love even as we are selflessly giving ourselves in what can nonetheless be very genuine loving. The habit—the abiding commitment—to love God must darken, empty, and completely cleanse the will. Or to look at it another way, love must liberate the will from the disordered desires that have held it enslaved. In what seems like a paradox, the gift of love must liberate our wills precisely so that we can truly love.

But What Is Love?

Perhaps it seems ironic that the Doctor of Mystical Love does not offer us a treatise on love. He does not reflect on types of love or analyze different words in Latin or Greek that can be used to speak of love.[5] John's principal concern is the love of God. Certainly, characteristic of Spanish mystical writers of his age, his language of love is often highly affective. This is clearer in the poetry, in *The Spiritual Canticle*, and in *The Living Flame of Love*. But John is not really speaking about an emotional or "felt" love. He says that the nurturing of such feelings of love is important to promote the devotion and strengthen the commitment of beginners. But the affective language that John uses when describing the experience of those who are more advanced in the spiritual journey portrays a different level of longing, desire, and self-giving.

4. Ruiz, *Introducción a San Juan de la Cruz*, 464.

5. C. S. Lewis offers the classic discussion of four types of love (affection, friendship, eros, and charity/agape) in *The Four Loves* (San Diego: Harcourt Brace Jovanovich, 1960).

To say that God loves us is to say that God offers the divine life to us. God's love is overflowing, self-giving, and other directed. It contains within itself an invitation to respond with a similar love in order to enter into a true mutuality and communion. Since it is quite impossible for us unaided to love God in return and to enter into such true mutuality, God gives us the gift of love, a sharing in the divine loving. God gives the divine self to us and then invites—and enables—us to give ourselves us in return. Ultimately, in divine union this will mean participating in the loving communion of the Trinity itself, loving God with God's own love within the life of God. As John of the Cross teaches us, in union, "her intellect [the soul's] will be the intellect of God, her will then will be God's will, and thus her love will be God's love. . . . The two wills are so united that there is only one will and love, which is God's" (C.38.3).

According to John, the love for God that purifies the will is not so much a *feeling* of love as we experience it in merely human terms. It is rather the deeper experience of longing for—or incompleteness without—the communion to which God invites us. It is the yearning to give ourselves fully and completely to God and thus to enter into divine communion. God offers us the divine life, God's very self, and God draws us to give ourselves completely in return. To love God truly is to long for, to choose, to be completely dedicated to giving ourselves totally to God from the deepest reality of our being so that we can enter into the unimaginable communion to which God invites us. Disordered desire and a will that is distracted, attached, enslaved stand in the way, so God gives us the theological virtue of love to empower us. John can speak of this deeper loving as a kind of spiritual "feeling," deeper than our usual experience of the emotion of love.

The active work of cultivating the theological virtue of love is a challenge. The work of ordering our desire is a difficult task indeed. Such love is not an emotion. Because of our sinfulness and disorder, it is a decision, a commitment, and a habitual resolve to forget self, to act for others, to give to God when we are tempted to serve ourselves. Again, the theological virtue of love is given in the *active* night of spirit, and it necessarily requires our graced effort.

In a world of sin, God's self-giving love inviting us into communion manifested itself in the form of the cross, in the total self-giving of the Second Person of the Trinity. Since humankind was unable to respond because of sin, God once again accomplished for us what we could not accomplish for ourselves. Our "no" to God, manifest in the rejection, betrayal, denial, and crucifixion of Jesus, was met by God's eternal "yes" to us nonetheless. The "yes" of the divine and human Jesus on the cross made it possible once again for all of us to raise up—and live out—our own "yes." Because we are sinners, our affirmation in love to the divine offer of love involves the hard work of embracing the gift. It calls on us, invites us, with God's continuing grace, to strengthen the gift of love at work within us.

For Questions for Reflection / Discussion see pages 157–158

7 Love's Still Deeper Liberation

The present work is designed as a general introduction to the Christian journey as taught by St. John of the Cross. But its particular focus has been the active work of emptying, purifying, darkening, or liberating discussed in the previous chapters. Most probably the *active* nights of sense and of spirit are more properly the material for a moral theologian like me. But John of the Cross never conceived of the work of the active nights as sufficient—as if, at their completion (to the degree that we can speak of them as ever being fully accomplished), we could just rest on our laurels and relax. The active nights are only part of a larger endeavor, the ascent to the peak of Mount Carmel, life-transforming union with God, and participation in the divine life itself. We cannot understand the spiritual itinerary laid out by the Mystical Doctor, nor can we fully understand the active nights themselves, without continuing, in a broad way, to look at the path that lies ahead.

The Four Nights

The journey of our inner liberation requires perseverance in the active work of purifying our desiring as well as purifying the intellect, the will, and the memory. We are never truly the principal agents of this work. The Catholic tradition, following St. Augustine, teaches that we are not capable of any good action without the impetus of God's grace. This is certainly true in the very difficult work of purgation. Still, in the two "nights" that we have examined thus far, we feel as though we are the principal agents, the ones doing all the work. The reality is that God has been helping us all along, but it is our effort and our struggle to grow in discipline that has been our immediate experience. But the time comes when God must more clearly and powerfully become the agent of our further journeying. We must enter the passive nights of sense and of spirit.

Before we continue, we need to recognize that the four nights—the *active* nights of sense and of spirit, and the *passive* nights of sense and of spirit—do unfold, in some way, like stages or phases that we pass through. At the different points of our journey, our focus is more exterior or interior, and we experience ourselves as more active or as more evidently receptive. There is a type of progression. At the same time, at least until union with God is deep and abiding, there is still an active purgation of the senses going on even in the passive nights since the roots of their disorder lie deeper within the person. ("The real purgation of the senses begins with spirit" [N.2.3.1].) God acting in us as the principal agent is inviting us to let go and to surrender more deeply, more completely. So the four nights are not completely distinct and progressive.

John of the Cross explains the two passive nights in *The Dark Night*, which is a kind of second volume to the reflection he began in *The Ascent*. Book 1 of *The Dark Night* is devoted to the passive night of sense, and book 2 to the passive night of spirit, which is perhaps what most people are thinking of when they speak of "the dark night" that John describes.

Thus, John of the Cross discusses the two *active* nights—in which human action is predominant—in *The Ascent of Mount Carmel*. He then continues with the two *passive* nights—in which divine action predominates—in *The Dark Night*. This logical arrangement, however, does not coincide exactly with their normal unfolding in life. In a more chronological, step-by-step presentation, we could say that the active work of purifying the senses, conforming our desires to our love for God (the active night of sense), is followed by the introduction of the first touches of the gift of contemplation. This new form of prayer and deeper encounter with God causes dryness and the absence of spiritual feeling (the passive night of sense). At the same time, the person begins actively to cooperate with God by embracing the gift of the theological virtues, bringing this liberating work to a deeper level (the active night of spirit). This sets the stage, at last, for God to work the deepest liberation in the passive night of spirit. Thus, while acknowledging that the divine and human are active in each level and that these are not absolutely separable stages, we can see that the two nights of sense, active and passive, precede the two nights of spirit, active and passive.

The Imperfections of Beginners

Early in his discussion of the passive night of sense in book 1 of *The Dark Night*, John devotes several chapters to the "imperfections of beginners" (at this point, especially "beginners" in the contemplative/mystical life). He identifies these imperfections with the traditional "seven capital vices," or what are sometimes called the "seven deadly sins": pride, avarice, lust, anger, gluttony, envy, and sloth. At first glance, this might seem a digression from the focus on God's continuing and deepening work of liberation. However, it is, in fact, an exposition of the deeper roots of our imperfection and sin that are in need of God's purifying action. Furthermore, in the course of his reflection on these imperfections, John provides many marvelous insights and counsels to assist us in our ongoing ascent. Although he speaks of these as the faults of *beginners*, surely every serious Christian, at virtually any stage, will find cause to nod and sadly smile at seeing himself or herself mirrored in John's descriptions. If John weren't so spot on, this discussion would almost seem like comic relief amid the deepening reflection on the experience of the dark night. Before moving to a look at the work of the passive night of sense, it would be helpful to look more closely at John's purposes in reflecting on these spiritual vices.

By the sixteenth century, the seven capital vices were a well-known list of evil dispositions that needed to be purified in any developing Christian life. Beginning with the work of fourth-century Evagrius Ponticus (346–399) and his disciple John Cassian (360–435) and then passed on to the Christian West through St. Gregory the Great (540–604), these dispositions have also been spoken of as the "seven deadly sins."[1] There is nonetheless a nuance of difference between the terms "vice" and "sin." John uses the term "vice," implying that while these imperfections are the result of our sinful condition, they are in themselves habitual dispositions or abiding tendencies rather than a generalized condition of separation from God or individual acts against God's will. They are dispositions opposed to virtues, and they move us to decisions and actions that weaken or contradict our efforts to grow in that inner liberation by which we can love God as completely as we ought. In fact, they are called "capital" vices—based on the Latin word meaning "head"—because they are the source (like "headwaters" of a great river) of other imperfections, vices, and sins. Further, in the context of

---

1. A very helpful historical review and contemporary discussion of these vices is provided by Rebecca Konyndyk DeYoung, *Glittering Vices: A New Look at the Seven Deadly Sins and Their Remedies* (Grand Rapids, Mich.: Brazos Press, 2009).

John's reflection, they are *spiritual* vices rather than *moral* vices, as they are normally considered in the tradition. Lust, gluttony, avarice, and the other moral vices would have been addressed in the active night of the senses (though not completely—at the root—since this liberation from vice is possible precisely by the deeper purgations that follow). John has taken up the discussion of capital vices as a tool to analyze more closely a deeper disorder in need of purgation.

In a particular way, these spiritual vices stand as obstacles to God's action in the passive night of sense, characterized by the dryness and aridity that arise when God withdraws the felt experience of consolation in prayer and introduces the gift of contemplation. Early in the spiritual life, as beginners, many Christians find joy in spiritual practices, in penance and devotions, and spiritual conversation with others. It is precisely this spiritual gratification that motivates us, and it is the withdrawal of these consolations that reveals our imperfections and thus the obstacles to be faced and overcome by God's purifying action and our cooperation with it. The capital vices, in this spiritual form, are various manifestations of a kind of deeper spiritual selfishness or self-centeredness that must be eradicated if the Christian is to embrace this newer and deeper form of prayer and relationship with God.

This is not the place to summarize all of the content of John's discussion of these imperfections. One noted commentator has argued that the two central vices in John's analysis are spiritual pride and spiritual gluttony, and the other five are rooted in those two (anger and envy being related to pride; and avarice, sloth, and lust related to gluttony).[2] Still, some discussion of

---

2. Federico Ruiz Salvador, *Místico y maestro: San Juan de la Cruz* (Madrid: Editorial de Espiritualidad, 2006), 342.

what John has to say will highlight the distinctive task of the purgation in the passive night of sense as well as point to some true jewels of spiritual insight that John has to offer.[3]

John begins his exposition with the vice traditionally considered to be the root of all the rest, namely, pride. His descriptions here are particularly incisive. Christians who have devoted themselves to prayer and have begun to reap its fruits in what they consider "good prayer experiences" and who have worked hard to order their desires now often face another failing: they become self-satisfied and proud:

> Then they develop a somewhat vain—at times very vain—desire to speak of spiritual things in others' presence, and sometimes even to instruct rather than be instructed; in their hearts they condemn others who do not seem to have the kind of devotion they would like them to have, and sometimes they give expression to this criticism like the pharisee who despised the publican while he boasted and praised God for the good deeds that he himself had accomplished. (N.1.2.1)

We might imagine their—or our own—sense of smugness and satisfaction. They may want themselves to be the only ones to appear holy. They want their spiritual guides to regard them with esteem. If this is lacking, they might seek out a guide who is more likely to provide the praise they think they deserve. They may hide their faults by confessing to priests other than their regular confessor (who would know them better). It's no wonder that such a vice, so typical of many serious Christians

---

3. Although the use of the capital vices provides a handy structure to examine the imperfections of beginners, it does not entirely fit John's purposes. Perhaps this is most clear in his discussion of the spiritual vice of lust (N.1.4), which is not so neatly transposed from a moral vice (and "sin of the flesh") to a spiritual vice.

at some stage, is an obstacle to God's introduction of a new form of prayer that is not based on their own efforts and that does not yield sweet feelings. God must free us of this vice of pride if we are to accept the gift of contemplation that God wants to give us and that is essential to continuing progress on the ascent.

Our own response to pride, in cooperation with the divine action, is the utterly essential and foundational virtue of humility (N.1.2.6–8). We are debtors to God who is the source of any good in us. We have much more ground to cover on this journey that leads to the peak. We are just beginners, blessed by God's call, helped by the divine grace, but in need of far more divine assistance for the path ahead.

It is in the course of speaking of the vice of spiritual pride that John offers a critical insight into the discouragement that many devoted Christians may feel in the face of their failures: "Sometimes they minimize their faults, and at other times they become discouraged by them, since they felt that they were already saints, and they become impatient and angry with themselves, which is yet another fault" (N.1.2.5). Isn't John wisely telling us that discouragement in the spiritual life is a sign of pride—a sign that we thought progress depended primarily on ourselves, on our own efforts, and on our ability to succeed spiritually? In fact, discouragement is a powerful and subtle enemy in the spiritual life—a powerful weapon in the devil's arsenal for those who are sincerely devoted if misguided. John's proposed remedy? "When they see themselves fall into imperfections, they suffer this with humility, with docility of spirit, and with loving fear of God and hope in him" (N.1.2.8). In short, they pick themselves up, with God's help and with trust in God's mercy, and they set out again—hopefully having learned again that they must lean on God's ever-present gracious help rather than relying on themselves.

Related to spiritual pride is the vice of anger (N.1.5). Beginners become angry over the faults of others or angry at their own: "Others, in becoming aware of their own imperfections grow angry with themselves in an unhumble impatience. So impatient are they about these imperfections that they want to become saints in a day" (N.1.5.3). Again, who has not wanted to be a saint or a contemplative, figuratively speaking, in a day! But this is not merely the naive idealism of beginners; it is an obstacle both to the work that lies ahead and to allowing God to act in us in ways that depend more on our docility than on our great abilities.

Spiritual envy too is related to the imperfection of pride. Rather than rejoicing in the virtues and gifts of others, the beginner is envious, not wanting even to hear other persons praised for their goodness. This is far different from a positive kind of "holy envy" in which the person is filled with a greater desire to grow, following the model of goodness that she or he is happy to see realized in others (N.1.7.1).

The spiritual vice of avarice, like its moral counterpart, is about acquisitiveness: wanting to collect, gather, and possess more—though, at this stage, it concerns acquisition of spiritual and religious things (N.1.3). Beginners want even more spiritual consolation. They also want more spiritual counsels, more spiritual books, more devotional images, more rosaries—more of the externals of religion—all to make them feel more spiritual and more able to converse wisely about spiritual things. Again, if John weren't so accurate, his description of a tendency many of us share would be comical. Who has not, at some point, almost become a "hoarder" in our accumulation of spiritual books, books on prayer, versions of the Bible, devotional images? It is so much more satisfying to acquire and enjoy such externals than to engage the sometimes hard work of prayer. It's so much more enjoyable to collect these spiritual things than to endure the aridity of the passive night of sense![4]

Beginners beset with the vice of spiritual gluttony crave sweetness in prayer like one afflicted with the moral vice craves sweet foods. They "desire to feel God and taste him as if he were comprehensible and accessible" (N.1.6.5)—while the path of dark faith is precisely moving us to embrace the utter incomprehensibility and transcendence of God. Christians afflicted with this particular vice, John says, "think the whole matter of prayer consists in looking for sensory satisfaction and devotion" (N.1.6.6). In *The Ascent*, John speaks of a kind of "spiritual sweet tooth" with which, avoiding the dryness that is the threshold to a deeper encounter with God, the person looks for one consoling prayer experience after another. Rather than truly seeking an encounter with God, on God's terms, the person is really seeking his or her own satisfaction at a different level (A.2.7.5). Elsewhere, John says pointedly, "The fly that clings to honey hinders its flight, and the soul that allows itself attachment to spiritual sweetness hinders its own liberty and contemplation" (SLL.24; see also Pre 17; Lt 13). This is the heart of the purgation that must occur in this passive night of sense if we are to embrace the dark knowing that is contemplation. Can't we all recognize ourselves in John's descriptions?

John last mentions the vice of sloth—offering a helpful summary of the reason we must be purified by God of all of these imperfections if we are to embrace the dark faith that is contemplation: "These beginners usually become weary in exercises that are more spiritual and flee from them since these exercises are contrary to sensory satisfaction. Since they are so used to finding

---

4. John offers detailed and lengthy counsel on the use of images and devotions (A.3.35–45).

delight in spiritual practices, they become bored when they do not find it" (N.1.7.2). How easy it is for us to give up on our prayer and spiritual discipline once it no longer offers us the consolation that we crave! John's words ring true: "Many of these beginners want God to desire what they want, and they become sad if they have to desire God's will. . . . They measure God by themselves and not themselves by God" (N.1.7.3).

Having offered his insightful reflections on these imperfections of beginners, John of the Cross reminds his readers that he has done so in order to highlight the work that God must now do in the passive night of sense. Here God leads the beginner more deeply into the dark night: "There, through pure dryness and interior darkness, he weans them from the breasts of these gratifications and delights, takes away all these trivialities and childish ways, and makes them acquire the virtues by very different means. No matter how earnestly beginners in all their actions and passions practice the mortification of self, they will never be able to do so entirely—far from it—until God accomplishes it in them passively by means of the purgation of this night" (N.1.7.5).

The liberation that occurs during this phase of night is principally God's work in us; yet, as John says at the start of his discussion of the imperfections of beginners, we have our part to play too: "But people should insofar as possible strive to do their part in purifying and perfecting themselves and thereby merit God's divine cure. In this cure God will heal them of what through their own efforts they were unable to remedy. No matter how much individuals do through their own efforts, they cannot actively purify themselves enough to be disposed in the least degree for the divine union of the perfection of love. God must take over and purge them in that fire that is dark for them" (N.1.3.3).

Having briefly examined these imperfections, we can now look more directly at God's action in the passive night of sense.

The Passive Night of Sense

The passive night of sense is the experience of darkness that comes upon us with the beginnings of contemplation. God is giving the gift of contemplation, but we are not yet acclimated to it. We experience God's closeness as dryness, aridity. The true reality of God cannot be experienced in the senses; thus, the gift of contemplation leaves these senses arid and empty. The person has been faithfully and actively engaged in prayer, but now God withdraws good feelings ("consolations") in prayer—or really, the divine presence bypasses normal feeling. We no longer "feel" God's presence, no longer "experience" the presence of God in prayer, no matter how much we redouble the effort in prayer or try new techniques or devotions. We feel dryness and absence, yet this is a gift of God and a sign of the invitation to take the next step. An important image that John uses here is that of a loving mother who must gently nudge her child into the next stage of growth:

> God nurtures and caresses the soul, after it has been resolutely converted to his service, like a loving mother who warms her child with the heat of her bosom, nurses it with good milk and tender food, and carries and caresses it in her arms. But as the child grows older, the mother withholds her caresses and hides her tender love; she rubs bitter aloes on her sweet breast and sets the child down from her arms, letting it walk on its own feet so that it may put aside the habits of child-hood and grow accustomed to greater and more important things. (N.1.1.2)

The praying person has faithfully engaged in the active work of inner liberation—ordering desire and darkening the faculties—so that, at last, there is space for the gift of contemplation. At first, almost unperceived because of its newness, one enters by God's gift into a quiet prayer of contemplation. The experience of dryness is the result of the inflow of God—a secret, hidden, loving knowledge of God that is unrecognizable to the senses and thus experienced as absence and dryness. God "fires the soul in the spirit of love," though as yet this most profound of loves is not "experienced" at all! God has enflamed a deeper burning of love that will slowly consume what is not yet of God, engulf the willing soul in the union of love, and flare out in intense love. The fire of divine love, of which John speaks here, will be the focus of *The Living Flame of Love*, which describes the life-transforming union with and into the God of love.

John of the Cross, ever the spiritual guide, describes three signs by which one may know that it is time to move beyond more active forms of prayer, to allow the gift of contemplation to take root and grow (N.1.9; A.2.13; SLL.119). It is possible, after all, to feel dryness at any moment on the journey of prayer—often enough caused, not by the invitation to contemplation, but by our lack of attention to prayer, halfheartedness, lukewarmness, or sin. Succinctly stated in *The Sayings of Light and Love*, "There are three signs of inner recollection: first, a lack of satisfaction in passing things; second, a liking for solitude and silence, and an attentiveness to all that is more perfect; third, the considerations, meditations and acts that formerly helped the soul now hinder it, and it brings to prayer no other support than faith, hope, and love" (SLL.119). They are all signs that God is drawing the person away from the exterior and superficial into union with the divine reality.

According to John, many reach this threshold (N.1.8.4), but because of lack of good spiritual guidance or knowledge of what is happening, they often try to force themselves back into yet more active prayer. John's appraisal here is a vitally important insight for those who desire to enter more deeply into the way of prayer. Once one begins praying, it's easy to focus attention on and expend energy on having good "experiences" in prayer—and in fact some religious movements, prayer groups, and books encourage this emphasis on experiences. How many Christians have actually been subtly invited into contemplative prayer and ultimately into union with God, at least in a transitory way, but failed to recognize the signs and the invitation? John's counsel is firm: do not go back! If the signs are present, do not try to force yourself back into your former ways of praying! This would be like "someone who turns from what has already been done in order to do it again, or like one who leaves a city only to re-enter it, or . . . like a hunter who abandons the prey in order to go hunting again. It is useless, then, for the soul to try to meditate because it will no longer profit by this exercise" (N.1.10.1). Rather, he urges those who find themselves at this threshold, "They must be content simply with a loving and peaceful attentiveness to God, and live without the concern, without the effort, and without the desire to taste or feel him" (N.1.10.4).

The dryness that comes with the initial gift of contemplation reminds us that ultimately we are not seeking an *experience* of God but rather a deep *encounter* with God in the divine reality itself. This has been the pattern, as we have seen in earlier chapters; everything that is not God or whatever is less than God must be left behind. Sweet feelings in prayer are infinitely less than God or a true encounter with the divine. Given the first experiences of true contemplation, we must embrace the dryness that accompanies this great gift of God precisely as we have been challenged to embrace the darkening, the emptying, the letting go along the way. The "one thing necessary" on this journey to the peak of Mount Carmel has nothing to do with feelings but is rather the surrender of self that makes it possible for God to give us an infinitely more genuine encounter and ultimately communion with the triune God. He concludes, "Accordingly, I would not consider any spirituality worthwhile that wants to walk in sweetness and ease and run from the imitation of Christ" (A.2.7.8).

Although the felt experience is one of dryness and absence, to receive the gift of contemplation is really to receive the divine presence: "For contemplation is nothing else than a secret and peaceful and loving inflow of God, which, if not hampered, fires the soul in the spirit of love" (N.1.10.6). This inflow and fire of love is not felt at the beginning, though at times it flows out into a sense of urgent longing for God. Divine love is at work so that, even in the midst of emptiness and darkness, "a habitual care and solicitude for God accompanied by grief or fear about not serving him" grows within the person (N.1.11.2). Again, this very solicitude and longing amidst the dryness is precisely one of the signs that God is drawing the person into union.

God is at work, purifying and liberating the person from within, and John points to the fruits of this difficult and trying time: self-knowledge and the growth in virtues to counter the imperfections, the spiritual vices, that beset beginners. Through the experience of darkness and emptiness, we come to see ourselves more clearly in our need and in our true distance from God (N.1.12). We come to recognize more clearly that God is truly grander and more transcendent than we had previously known, and we come to recognize as well our own smallness and need: "We conclude that self-knowledge flows first from this dry night, and that from this knowledge as from its source proceeds the other knowledge of God" (N.1.12.5). In short, the experience of darkness and dryness yields a truer humility, which, as we have already seen, is the foundational remedy for the imperfections of beginners. John devotes a chapter to noting the effects of the painful gift of this darkness on efforts to overcome each of the spiritual vices (N.1.13).

The soul has now passed through the active night of sense, which largely calms and orders our desires (*Ascent*, book 1); the passive night of sense in which we surrender to the inflow of divine love experienced as darkness (*Night*, book 1); and the emptying of the intellect, memory, and will in the active night of spirit (*Ascent*, books 2 and 3). The person can now say, in the words of the poem *The Dark Night*, "My house being now all stilled" (N.1.13.15).

The Passive Night of Spirit

The passive night of spirit is the necessary completion of the divine and human work of liberation that has gone before, because all of our sins and imperfections have deeper roots within us: "The difference between the two purgations is like the difference between pulling up roots or cutting off a branch, rubbing out a fresh stain or an old, deeply embedded one. As we have said, the purgation of the senses is only the gate to and beginning of contemplation that leads to the purgation of spirit" (N.2.2.1). All that has gone before has really brought the external, the material, and the sensory into conformity with the interior and the spiritual—"the accommodation of the senses to the spirit" (N.2.2.1). With the purgation of the spirit, the deeper purgation of the senses can actually occur, so John concludes, "The real purgation of the senses begins with the spirit. Hence the night of the senses . . . should be called a certain reformation and bridling of the appetite rather than a purgation. The reason is that all of the imperfections and disorders of the sensory part are rooted in the spirit and from it receive their strength" (N.2.3.1).

In the passive night of spirit—the "dark night" at its most profound depth—God works to purify the deepest reality of the person, beneath the senses: "He leaves the intellect in darkness, the will in aridity, the memory in emptiness, and the affections in supreme affliction, bitterness, and anguish," and God does so "by means of a pure and dark contemplation" (N.2.3.3). "For," John tells us, "the sensory part is purified by aridity, the faculties by the void of their apprehensions, and the spirit by thick darkness" (N.2.6.4).

The dark night of spirit is, in fact, contemplation, the inflow of God who both purges and illuminates the person who waits in nakedness and poverty of spirit. The darkness is the blindness that comes with excessive light because "the divine light of contemplation . . . causes spiritual darkness" (N.2.5.3). God is, in fact, so present to the person at his or her depth that it causes misery in a soul that is not yet fully emptied and pure. The pain is caused not by contemplation itself but by the remaining imperfections that are not compatible with the presence of God (N.2.9.11).

The profound encounter with God in a deepening and more sustained contemplation manifests ever more deeply to the soul the deep roots of sin. It is as if a bright light reveals smudges and imperfections not previously noted. The darkness and suffering of this night include the temptation to feel that separation from God is the inevitable consequence of one's sins, which have become more evident to the person than ever before—though one's companions might, at the same time, be praising him or her as a great saint. To see and to face the reality of our sins is a great, if sometimes painful, grace at any moment on the Christian journey. By it we are given new reason to wonder at God's merciful love as well as new reason to repent. Here in the dark night of spirit, the ugly reality of one's sin is so clear that the person is tempted to doubt that God would ever love such a sinner. John of the Cross expressly compares this painful purgation to the suffering of the souls in purgatory—a comparison that provides real theological insight into the final process of purification that Catholics believe occurs even after death (N.2.12).

In reviewing the passive night of sense, with its characteristic dryness, we noted that the inflow of God in the first contemplative encounters brings with it an enflaming of the soul with love, though it is experienced at that point as an urgent longing. Here too in the passive night of spirit, even more, the inflow of God enkindles a still deeper fire of love and a still more intense longing in the midst of the terrible feeling of absence. With this longing, at a level very different from our normal ways of experiencing feelings, comes a strength to persevere and a spiritual boldness, even in the midst of a profound sense of unworthiness and darkness (N.2.13).

The Log and the Flame

One of the central images used by John of the Cross provides a superb summary of the entire process of liberation leading to divine union, which we have been examining in the previous chapters: the log and the flame (A.1.11.6; A.2.8.2; N.2.10.1–9; N.2.11.1; F.Prol.3; F.1.3–4, 19–25, 33). John provides one of his most extended and yet still concise uses of this image in discussing the passive night of spirit:

The soul is purged and prepared for union with the divine light just as the wood is prepared for transformation into fire. Fire, when applied to wood, first dehumidifies it, dispelling all moisture and making it give off any water it contains. Then it gradually turns the wood black, makes it dark and ugly, and even causes it to emit a bad odor. By drying out the wood, the fire brings to light and expels all those ugly and dark accidents that are contrary to fire. Finally, by heating and enkindling it from without, the fire transforms the wood into itself and makes it as beautiful as it is itself. Once transformed, the wood no longer has any activity or passivity of its own, except for its weight and its quantity which is denser than the fire. It possesses the properties and performs the actions of fire: It is dry and it dries; it is hot and it gives off heat; it is brilliant and it illumines; it is also much lighter in weight than before. It is the fire that produces all these properties in the wood. (N.2.10.1)

The various stages of purification appear to be the negative effects of a log set aflame, but ultimately the log becomes one with the flame. Here we can picture the way a hot blue flame seems to dance and flicker from within the very substance of the log that has been burning for a long while. This latter stage is an image for union in which the purified person is so united with God that God is the principal agent acting within the person. The person knows, loves, and acts by God's action: "This renovation illumines the human intellect with supernatural light so it becomes divine, united with the divine; informs the will with love of God so it is no longer less than divine and loves in no other way than divinely, united and made one with the divine will and love. . . . And thus this soul will be a soul of heaven, heavenly and more divine than human" (N.2.13.11).

It is precisely by passing through this last night, allowing God to accomplish this painful but necessary purification in us, that the soul is able to surrender completely to the contemplation that God had already been giving. The soul is liberated from itself; it is accommodated to the divine presence. Night gives way to day; the dark night, to the light of divine union and ultimately the light of glory in the world to come.

For Questions for Reflection / Discussion see page 158

8 Love's Pinnacle

In *The Ascent of Mount Carmel* and *The Dark Night*, John of the Cross focuses his attention on the dark but liberating path that leads to the summit, which is nothing less than loving union with God. Although arduous, the journey begins with love for God, is awakened by encounter with the divine love, and, with the inflow of love in contemplation, is sustained by love. But it is in his other two extant books, *The Spiritual Canticle* and *The Living Flame of Love*, that the centrality of love in the thought of John of the Cross becomes utterly and emphatically clear. No wonder that many commentators urge those readers who are encountering John's works for the first time to begin with one of these latter books.

In *The Spiritual Canticle*, John of the Cross comments on the poem of the same title, a song of the soul yearning with love for the Beloved, who has wounded the soul with love and who is also wounded with love for the soul. The central imagery here is bridal and marital: John focuses on the "spiritual betrothal" of the soul with God and, ultimately, on the "spiritual marriage," the union of the now-transformed soul with God. (As hard as it is to imagine, John wrote the first thirty-one stanzas of this sublime love poem during his grueling nine-month imprisonment in a Toledo prison cell!)

In *The Living Flame of Love*, John's commentary on the poem unfolds the image of the log and the flame, which he had explained in *The Dark Night*. But now the focus is no longer on the purifying role of the flame but on how the log, transformed into fire, sends forth flames of intense love for God. This is his account of the deepest experience of union with God possible in this life, the soul's participation in the triune life of God. It is a description of love's intensity as well as a song of praise for the working in the soul of the three Persons of the Trinity.

The Spiritual Canticle and Bridal Mysticism

The Ascent of Mount Carmel and *The Dark Night* focus on the journey of dark faith. *The Spiritual Canticle* too focuses on the journey, though now explicitly as the pursuit of loving union with God who has awakened this love in the soul but who stands now beyond the soul's vision and its grasping. The poem begins,

> Where have you hidden,
> Beloved, and left me moaning?
> you fled like the stag
> after wounding me;
> I went out calling you, but you were gone. (C.1)

The lovesick soul sets out, refusing to be distracted or waylaid by the beauty of created things and wanting no more messengers but only the Beloved himself. (Doesn't that describe, although in far different terms, what the previous discussions of purgation have really meant?) The Beloved, like a "wounded stag," yearns too for the soul (C.13.9). The poem takes on the form of a loving dialogue between the soul and the Beloved. John speaks of God's yearning for us with a similar image in another of his poems:

> A lone young shepherd lived in pain
> withdrawn from pleasure and contentment,

his thoughts fixed on a shepherd-girl
his heart an open wound with love.

    Stanzas applied spiritually to Christ and the soul, stanza 1

Following on the focus of the lover seeking the beloved, John of the Cross uses bridal imagery to describe the intimate union of the person and God. The soul in the poem is called the Bride, and the Beloved is the Bridegroom. In marriage, after all, "two become one flesh," and a deeper union between persons could hardly be imagined. John is by no means unique within the Christian tradition in finding such imagery in the Hebrew Scripture's Song of Songs (as well as in other texts of both the Old and New Testaments: Is 54:5; Hos 2:19; Ez 16:8; 2 Cor 11:2; Eph 5:25; Rev 19:7-9, 21:2; 22:17). Beginning with Origen in the third century through such famous saintly mystics as Bernard of Clairvaux in the twelfth, the thirteenth-century Gertrude the Great, Catherine of Siena in the four-teenth century, and John's contemporary Teresa of Avila, the union of the soul with God has been understood according to the image of a man and a woman passing from mere attraction, through courtship, to betrothal and finally to marriage—the longing for intimate and lasting union growing ever stronger along the way.

In union, God gives the divine life itself to the soul, with a love beyond our imagining (C.27.1): "In this interior union God communicates himself to the soul with such genuine love that neither the affection of a mother, with which she so tenderly caresses her child, nor a brother's love, nor any friendship is comparable to it." In this divine self-giving in love, we witness God's incredible humility toward the human person, which is "as though he were her servant and she his lord. And he is as solicitous in favoring her as he would be if he were her slave and she his god. So profound is the humility and sweetness of God." John then breaks out in an exclamation of wonder: "O wonderful thing, worthy of all our awe and admiration!"

Yet the emphasis is on not only the union but also the transformation that occurs in the person: "The soul thereby becomes divine, God through participation, insofar as is possible in this life" (C.22.3). "The union wrought between the two natures and the communication of the divine to the human in this state is such that even though neither changes its being, both appear to be God" (C.22.4). The soul "has been transformed into her God" (C.22.4). Such is the union attained in the mutual surrender and mutual self-giving of the divine and the human.

The language of *The Spiritual Canticle* and of *The Living Flame of Love* is highly affective, but it must be noted that John is not talking about merely superficial feelings or emotions that can come and go. The yearning love of which he speaks here is not principally felt in the senses and emotions. Rather, it is a love that flows from the deepest being of the person, rooted in our radical incompleteness apart from God, our infinite capacity and yearning for communion with God, and God's own infinite love which now flows in and through the soul in union with the divine life. While it seems that this deeper, mystical love can best be understood by its parallel with a passionate, even sexual, love—and indeed it can overflow into the feelings and emotions—still, it is substantially different and more profound (C.25.9–11). John explains that the beginner's love for God is like the experience of new lovers whose affection is still a kind of superficial infatuation, while the love for God of more advanced souls is like that of more seasoned human lovers whose love is deeper, tested, and secure (C.25.10–11).

Participation in the Life of the Triune God

The sublime, ineffable nature of what John is trying to describe ultimately passes into mystery. John wants us to recognize that the transformation into God by participation in divine union is not some static, accomplished event. It is an entering into the eternal dynamism within the very life of the triune God:

> The Holy Spirit elevates the soul sublimely and informs her and makes her capable of breathing in God the same spiration of love that the Father breathes in the Son and the Son in the Father. This spiration of love is the Holy Spirit himself, who in the Father and the Son breathes out to her in this transformation in order to unite her to himself. There would not be a true and total transformation if the soul were not transformed in the three Persons of the Most Holy Trinity in an open and manifest degree. . . . Even what comes to pass in the communication given in this temporal transformation is unspeakable, for the soul united and transformed in God breathes out in God to God the very divine spiration that God—she being transformed in him—breathes out in himself to her. (C.39.3)

What John of the Cross is saying here is utterly incredible! The word "spiration" is a technical theological term to describe the inner relationship of the three Persons of the Trinity (inasmuch as we can speak of it at all). John is saying that in this deepest union, the mystical marriage, we will become intimate participants in the inner life of God! "The Blessed Trinity inhabits the soul by divinely illumining its intellect with the wisdom of the Son, delighting its will in the Holy Spirit, and absorbing it powerfully and mightily in the unfathomed embrace of the Father's sweetness" (F.1.15). The mysticism of John of the Cross is thus profoundly and essentially trinitarian.

If this invitation to participate in God's very life is offered to us who are sinful creatures and if this loving union awaits us at the pinnacle of the ascent of Mount Carmel—even though the way is steep, arduous, and dark—does it not make sense to risk everything to experience this supreme grace? In the light of this vision of the All (*Todo*), doesn't it make sense to let go of absolutely everything that is less than this (the *nada*)?

John of the Cross stands at the pinnacle, looking back at us, his brothers and sisters, his fellow pilgrims on the way—God seekers, yes, but distracted, wandering, struggling, blind, misguided. He beckons to us, invites us onward. The Mystical Doctor wants to show all of us the most direct and sure way to join him and all the saints where there is nothing (*nada*) other than sharing in the life of the triune God. Ultimately, as St. John of the Cross proclaims lyrically in his *Stanzas given a spiritual meaning:* with a consuming love and an unfaltering hope that will be fully satisfied only in the life to come, we can at last reach our goal—union with our God, our Lover and Beloved.

> I went out seeking love,
> and with unfaltering hope
> I flew so high, so high,
> that I overtook the prey.

For Questions for Reflection / Discussion see page 159

Questions for Reflection / Discussion

Introduction

1. Have you ever tried before to read a book by John of the Cross? If so, what was your experience of it?

2. If you haven't done so before, read a poem by John of the Cross—*The Dark Night* or *The Spiritual Canticle*, for example. (Or read it again if you did so in the past.) If you knew nothing else about him, what might the poem tell you about John of the Cross? Can you see why he has traditionally been called the "Doctor of Mystical Love"?

3. What is your interest in John of the Cross? What do you hope to discover—or how do you hope to grow—by becoming more familiar with his writing now?

4. How would you describe the relationship between your moral life (e.g., effort to avoid sin, do good, grow in virtues, love your neighbor, and grow in ongoing conversion) and your spiritual life (e.g., personal prayer, Scripture reading, common prayer, participation in the Eucharist, and other sacraments)? Can you see how strengthening one would strengthen the other?

5. Have you ever encountered the idea that growth in prayer requires growth in your moral life? How would immorality or sin hinder one's prayer?

6. Does it make sense to you to speak of the Christian life as a path of deeper liberation? In what ways could a modern person be un-free?

1 | St. John of the Cross: Life [Spiritual Itinerary]

1. The religious and cultural context in which John of the Cross lived greatly influenced his life and spirituality. How do you think that the context in which you live impacts, for good or ill, your own effort to grow in a deeper and more authentic relationship with God?

2. John of the Cross wrote soaring mystical love poetry under horrible circumstances while imprisoned by his Carmelite brothers. Have you experienced the presence of God in the midst of hard times in your life?

3. How would you describe the spiritual "itinerary" of your life up to this moment? As you look ahead, along what path do you think that God is leading you to walk?

4. Teresa of Avila classically described the Christian life as an inner journey to encounter God in the inmost chamber of an "interior castle"; John of the Cross too invites us to this inner journey to find God in the inner sanctuary of our soul. Do you experience God within yourself, as well as outside and beyond you? For example, as you are praying in the presence of Christ in the Blessed Sacrament (outside of yourself, in that sense), have you also experienced Christ deep within you?

5. Have you ever had an experience of wonder, beauty, love, or divine presence that was "ineffable"—that is, that you couldn't fully express in words? Or maybe so precious that you just didn't want to share it with others in words?

6. John of the Cross wrote for men and women who were "on fire" in their faith. He didn't feel much need for promoting devotion and zeal to his readers. He assumed it. Have you experienced such "fire" in yourself or others? If so, when?

When the popes today speak of the "new evangelization," how does it relate to being "on fire"?

2 | The Asceticism of the Ascent

1. The title of this book is *Love Awakened by Love*. It is an effort to express the foundation of the spirituality of John of the Cross. How would you explain "love awakened by love" as a manner of describing the Christian life and journey?

2. Have you ever been in love? Madly and "head over heels"? How might that experience help to make sense of the letting go that John of the Cross views as so essential?

3. Have you ever had to work and struggle to attain something that you really wanted—for example, an athletic, academic, or musical achievement? Was the sacrifice and effort worth it for you? How is that an analogy for the Christian life?

4. If we read the Gospels with fresh eyes, we see that Jesus is really quite demanding: deny yourself, take up the cross, lose your life, sell and give everything to the poor, and so forth. How do you make sense of such sayings? Is John of the Cross reading them too literally?

5. Do you experience yourself as "attached" to things or to people in a needy way? Do these attachments get in the way of your own growth as a person and as a Christian or in your relationship with others? How so?

6. Have you ever felt intensely God's love for you personally? When? Did that experience change you or your relationship with God?

7. Do you experience your love for God as a total, all-encompassing love? Do you love people and things in your life as much as, alongside, more than, or in place of God?

8. A lot of people today—even Christians—don't really think much about sin or about themselves as sinners. We can easily think that we just "make mistakes," but we don't really sin. We are, after all, basically good people. How do think that John of the Cross would respond to this popular sense of sin?

3 | The Theological Virtues

1. Contemporary moral theology focuses a lot of attention on virtues—habitual dispositions for the good. Have you ever thought of your own life in terms of your fundamental attitudes and virtues? What are some virtues that you admire most in other people and that you would aspire to attain? What vices—habitual dispositions that lead us to evil—do you think that you see in yourself or as prevalent in our culture?

2. Do you experience God's hand in your life, directing and strengthening you for the good? Do you think that you have experienced "infused" virtues—dispositions for the good that are the result of God's action rather than your own effort to grow in virtue?

3. How do you experience the presence of the theological virtues of faith, hope, and love in your own life? Where do you see them active?

4. Thomas Aquinas taught that we must have faith first—that is, we must first believe in God and in the divine love by which God invites us into friendship. Then, we can hope to attain that communion, and our love for God can be awakened. In another way, though, when we love God, our faith and hope grow stronger. What arrangement or order of faith, hope, and love makes the most sense in your own experience?

4 | Faith

1. How do you experience a "natural" faith? What, at a natural level, do you know by faith? How have you experienced faith in other people? Has your faith ever been disappointed?

2. Christian faith can be understood at a number of levels: as belief in God and in truths about God, as a relationship and trust in God, and as a virtue and a life commitment. How have you experienced faith at these levels?

3. Today, a lot of people will say, "I believe in God." They may live basically good lives, but their belief doesn't seem to have a lot of impact on their lives. Assuming that this is a kind of faith, what is incomplete about it? Why?

4. How has your faith—your knowledge of and your relationship with God—grown over the years? What have been the catalysts, the factors, that have promoted your growth in faith?

5. How have your images of God (as father or mother, as friend, as shepherd, or as protector, etc.) changed over the years? What is the image of God that seems to predominate in your life of prayer now? As useful as such images can be, John of the Cross says that we must move beyond them. Does that seem possible? Desirable?

6. We can say that God is both utterly immanent and utterly transcendent, that is, God is both intimately present to us and even within us and, at the same time, always infinitely beyond us. John of the Cross invites us to know this immanent and transcendent God through a "dark faith" that does not see or understand. Does that make sense to you? How would you explain this "dark faith" to someone else?

7. When have you been challenged to grow in a "dark faith"—challenged simply to wait and to trust? Did your faith grow stronger?

8. For John of the Cross, "dark faith," which is an obscure, loving knowledge of God, is closely related to contemplation, which is a wordless experience of God's presence. Have you experienced God's presence in an obscure, dark, but loving way?

5 | Hope

1. How have you experienced the negative power of memory? Do you have memories in need of healing? Have you ever been weighed down by the past—carried "baggage" from the past? Has it ever gotten in the way of moving forward in your life?

2. Christian faith brings us to believe in the eternal life that God invites us to share. How does our society promote or obstruct the growth of our hope of sharing in that gift of eternal life?

3. Have you ever felt really discouraged in life or even tempted to despair completely? What pulled you out of it?

4. What would it mean to say that someone has "presumed on our friendship or on our generosity"? What is wrong with such presumption? How can people be guilty of presumption in relationship with a God who is love?

5. John of the Cross sees a close connection between memory and imagination. What we imagine for the future is closely tied to what we have experienced or learned in the past. How is the connection between memory and imagination helpful to us? How is it an obstruction?

6. How do you experience hope in your life now? What do you hope for? How does that hope impact your daily living?

7. Have you experienced the connection between hoping to possess or achieve something and yearning for it—wanting something so much that you could almost taste it? How did that impact you?

6 | Love

1. Have you ever experienced a love awakened by love, that is, has someone else's love for you awakened or deepened your love for him or her?

2. Have you ever experienced a love that is not really selfless, that is, a "love" that is really about the person who is loving and not about the good of the object of that love? In other words, have you ever experienced a needy love?

3. Have you ever experienced obstacles within yourself to loving someone else? Have you ever wanted to love someone freely and generously but felt like something held you back? Or, on the other hand, have you ever desired the love of someone who could not love you in return because of some inner obstruction? How would that experience be like what John of the Cross is describing?

4. Has your love for someone ever led you to love what they love?

5. Has your love, desire, or need for something or someone ever gotten in your way of loving God?

6. Who in your own experience has exhibited a truly selfless love for you or for others? What would make you call it a "selfless" love?

7. What does it mean to say that love is not so much a feeling as it is an act of the will and a commitment? How, for example, might this understanding of love be evident in Christian

marriage? What, then, does it mean to love God and to be loved by God?

7 | Love's Still Deeper Liberation

1. Do you recognize yourself in any of the "imperfections of beginners" that John of the Cross describes?

2. Have you ever experienced spiritual discouragement—a sense of discouragement about your spiritual life, your ability to overcome sin, or your ability to live a good Christian life? Was that ultimately good or bad for your Christian journey? Was it a help or a hindrance?

3. John of the Cross's discussion of "spiritual gluttony" is part of his teaching against dependence on "consolations" (good feelings) in prayer. Have you been a "spiritual glutton"? Is it possible to have a life of prayer without consolations?

4. Have ever experienced "dryness" or "aridity" in prayer? To what did you attribute the experience?

5. John of the Cross teaches that dryness in prayer can be a sign of an invitation to contemplative prayer. In fact, he says that more people are probably invited to contemplative prayer than realize it. Do you think that you might have overlooked such an invitation in your own life of prayer up to now? What would John of the Cross invite you to consider?

6. How would you explain John of the Cross's concept of the "dark night"? What is the difference between the dark night and simply being depressed or experiencing hard times? Why is a dark night necessary? How is it liberating?

7. Explain John of the Cross's image of the log and flame as an illustration of the spiritual journey. Does it make sense? Is it a helpful illustration for people today?

8 | Love's Pinnacle

1. Have you ever felt "wounded" by love? Lovesick? Have you ever felt wounded by love for God? Have you ever considered that God might be wounded with love for you?

2. Have you seen a picture of the famous marble sculpture of St. Teresa of Avila in ecstasy by the Italian Baroque artist Bernini? It depicts St. Teresa swooning in ecstasy as an angel prepares to plunge an arrow of love into her heart. Look for the image on the Internet. How would you describe the emotion or experience that it depicts?

3. How does the image of "spiritual marriage" explain the experience of union between the soul and God? Can you think of other images that you might use to explain divine union (recalling that Christian doctrine requires that we maintain the distinction between God and the soul even while we say that they are in union)?

4. A lot of Christians probably don't give much serious thought to the doctrine of the Trinity—that God is One in Three Persons: Father, Son, and Spirit. Yet, John of the Cross, like many mystics, experiences it as central to communion with God. How does a person in union experience the Persons of the Trinity? How, for that matter, might Christians experience the Trinity in their own life and prayer?

Sketch of Mount Carmel (the Ascent) by St. John of the Cross

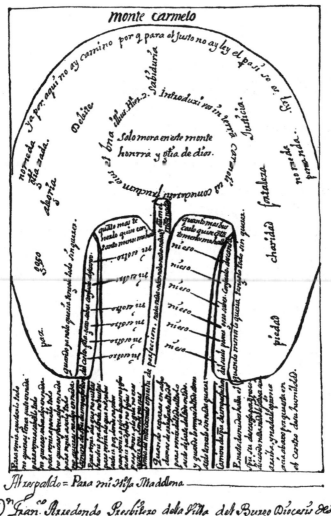

Spanish Original

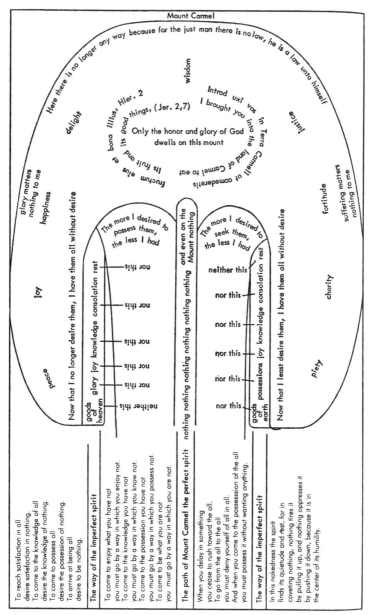

English rendering/translation

Bibliography

COLLECTED WORKS OF SAINT JOHN OF THE CROSS

The Collected Works of St. John of the Cross. Translated by Kieran Kavanaugh, O.C.D., and Otilio Rodriguez, O.C.D. Rev. ed. Washington, D.C.: ICS Publications, 1999.

The Complete Works of Saint John of the Cross. Translated and edited by E. Allison Peers from the critical edition of Silverio de Santa Teresa. New rev. ed. 3 vols. Westminster, Md.: Newman, 1953. Reprinted in one volume. New York: Sheed and Ward, 1978.

John of the Cross: Selected Writings. Edited with an introduction by Kieran Kavanaugh, O.C.D. Preface by Ernest Larkin, O.Carm. Classics of Western Spirituality. Mahwah, N.J.: Paulist, 1987.

St. John of the Cross: A Digital Library. CD-ROM. Washington, D.C.: ICS Publications, 2003. This CD-ROM includes the Spanish text of John's works, as well as the Kavanaugh-Rodriguez and the Peers translations; the Douay-Rheims translation of the Bible; and search tools.

SECONDARY SOURCES

Brennan, Gerald. *St. John of the Cross: His Life and Poetry.* Cambridge, England: Cambridge University Press, 1973.

Burrows, Ruth, O.C.D. *Ascent to Love: The Spiritual Teaching of St. John of the Cross.* Denville, N.J.: Dimension Books, 1987.

Collings, Ross, O.C.D. *John of the Cross.* Way of the Mystics 10. Collegeville, Minn.: Liturgical/Michael Glazier, 1990.

Crisógono de Jesús Sacramentado, O.C.D. *The Life of St. John of the Cross.* Translated by Kathleen Pond. London: Longmans, Green, 1958.

Cummins, Norbert, O.C.D. *Freedom to Rejoice: Understanding St. John of the Cross.* London: Harper Collins, 1991.

Dicken, E. W. Trueman. *The Crucible of Love: A Study of the Mysticism of St. Teresa and St. John of the Cross.* London: Darton, Longman, and Todd, 1963.

Doohan, Leonard. *The Contemporary Challenge of John of the Cross: An Introduction to His Life and Teaching.* Washington, D.C.: ICS Publications, 1995.

Dubay, Thomas, S.M. *Fire Within: St. Teresa of Avila, St. John of the Cross, and the Gospel on Prayer.* San Francisco: Ignatius Press, 1989.

Foley, Marc, O.C.D. *The Ascent of Mount Carmel: Reflections.* Washington, D.C.: ICS Publications, 2013.

Gabriel de Sainte-Marie Magdeleine, O.C.D. *St. John of the Cross: Doctor of Love and Contemplation.* Translated by a Benedictine of Stanbrook Abbey. Cork, Ireland: Mercier, 1947.

Hardy, Richard. *John of the Cross: Man and Mystic.* Boston: Pauline, 2004. (This is a revised and updated version of *Search for Nothing.*)

———. *Search for Nothing: The Life of John of the Cross.* New York: Crossroad, 1982.

Herrera, R. A. *Silent Music: The Life, Work, and Thought of St. John of the Cross.* Grand Rapids, Mich.: Eerdmans, 2004.

Howells, Edward. *John of the Cross and Teresa of Avila: Mystical Knowing and Selfhood.* New York: Crossroad, 2002.

Kavanaugh, Kieran, O.C.D. *John of the Cross: Doctor of Light and Love.* Spiritual Legacy Series. New York: Crossroad, 1999.

Matthew, Iain. *The Impact of God: Soundings from St. John of the Cross.* London: Hodder and Staughton, 1995.

Merton, Thomas. *Ascent to Truth.* New York: Harcourt Brace, 1951.

Muto, Susan. *John of the Cross for Today: The Ascent.* Notre Dame, Ind.: Ave Maria Press, 1991.

O'Donoghue, Noel. *Adventures in Prayer: Reflections on St. Teresa of Avila, St. John of the Cross, and St. Thérèse of Lisieux.* London: Burns and Oates, 2004.

Peers, E. Allison. *Handbook to the Life and Times of St. Teresa and St. John of the Cross.* Westminster, Md.: Newman, 1954.

———. *Spirit of Flame: A Study of St. John of the Cross*. New York: Morehouse-Graham, 1944.

Ruiz, Federico, O.C.D., ed., et al. *God Speaks in the Night: The Life, Times, and Teaching of St. John of the Cross*. Translated by Kieran Kavanaugh, O.C.D. Washington, D.C.: ICS Publications, 1991.

Simsic, Wayne. *Seeking the Beloved: A Prayer Journey with St. John of the Cross*. Frederick, Md.: The Word Among Us, 2012.

Stein, Edith. *The Science of the Cross*. Translated by Josephine Koeppel, O.C.D. Vol. 6, *The Collected Works of Edith Stein*. Edited by Dr. L. Gelber and Romaeus Leuven, O.C.D. Washington, D.C.: ICS Publications, 2002.

Tyler, Peter M. *St. John of the Cross*. New York: Continuum, 2010.

Welch, John, O.Carm. *When Gods Die: An Introduction to John of the Cross*. Mahwah, N.J.: Paulist, 1990.

Index

imprisonment and escape of,
20–21
life of, 14–22
"*nada*" doctrine of, 36
poetry of, 1, 6, 20–21, 22, 23,
30–31, 34, 49, 90, 112
preaching and, 21–22
prose works of, 1, 6, 22
spiritual itinerary and, 5, 25
spiritual life of, 19
themes of, ix–x, 1
tips for reading, 30–33
understanding, 1–2
writings of, ix, 20, 23–25,
30–33
*John of the Cross: Doctor of Light
and Love* (Kavanaugh), 2n1
Joseph, St., 2
Joy, 93, 116–19
disordered, 117–18
sinful, 104–5
Judaism, 15–17
Justice, 56

Kavanaugh, Kieran, 2n1, 13n1,
30n8

Laity, 16, 22
Lamentations, 96
Letter to the Colossians, 40
Liberation
active night of spirit and, 128
Christian life and, ix–x

contemplation and, 5
disordered desire and, 120–21
enslavements and, ix–x
faith and, 5
grace and, x, 28
hope and, 5, 103
log and the flame and, 142–44
love and, 4, 5, 43, 126–44
passive night of sense and, 10
passive night of spirit and, 10,
29, 128, 140
prayer and, 29, 137
purification and, 4, 5, 23, 43, 50
sin and, 4, 29, 128
spiritual journey and, 28–29
union with God and, 8, 11, 28,
37, 142
virtues and, x
of will, 54, 123
Liberty. *See* Liberation
The Life (St. Teresa of Avila), 19
The Living Flame of Love (St.
John of the Cross), 23–24, 27,
29, 30, 34, 67, 92, 111, 112,
123, 137, 145, 148
Log and the flame, 142–44,
145–46
Lonergan, Bernard, 37
Love, 4–5, 14, 60–61, 77, 121
active night of spirit and, 125
affections and, 112
asceticism and, 47–49
attachments and, 36, 43–47
desires and, 113–16, 116–19,
121–23

About Us

ICS Publications, based in Washington, D.C., is the publishing house of the Institute of Carmelite Studies (ICS) and a ministry of the Discalced Carmelite Friars of the Washington Province (U.S.A.). The Institute of Carmelite Studies promotes research and publication in the field of Carmelite spirituality, especially about Carmelite saints and related topics. Its members are friars of the Washington Province.

The Discalced Carmelites are a worldwide Roman Catholic religious order comprised of friars, nuns, and laity—men and women who are heirs to the teaching and way of life of Teresa of Avila and John of the Cross, dedicated to contemplation and to ministry in the church and the world.

Information about their way of life is available through local diocesan vocation offices, or from the Discalced Carmelite Friars vocation directors at the following addresses:

Washington Province:
1525 Carmel Road, Hubertus, WI 53033

California-Arizona Province:
P.O. Box 3420, San Jose, CA 95156

Oklahoma Province:
5151 Marylake Drive, Little Rock, AR 72206

Visit our websites at:
www.icspublications.org and *http://ocdfriarsvocation.org*